How to be Charismatic, Develop Confidence, and Exude Leadership

---

The Miracle Formula for Magnetic Charisma, Defeating Anxiety, and Winning at Communication

Richard Banks

How to be Charismatic & Develop Confidence

How to be Charismatic & Develop Confidence

© **Copyright 2020 by Richard Banks. All right reserved**
The content contained within this book may not be reproduced, duplicated or transmitted without direct written permission from the author or the publisher.

Under no circumstances will any blame or legal responsibility be held against the publisher, or author, for any damages, reparation, or monetary loss due to the information contained within this book. Either directly or indirectly.

Legal Notice:

This book is copyright protected. This book is only for personal use. You cannot amend, distribute, sell, use, quote or paraphrase any part, or the content within this book, without the consent of the author or publisher.

Disclaimer Notice:

Please note the information contained within this document is for educational and entertainment purposes only. All effort has been executed to present accurate, up to date, and reliable, complete information. No warranties of any kind are declared or implied. Readers acknowledge that the author is not engaging in the rendering of legal, financial, medical or professional advice. The content within this book has been derived from various sources. Please consult a licensed professional before attempting any techniques outlined in this book.

By reading this document, the reader agrees that under no circumstances is the author responsible for any losses, direct or indirect, which are incurred as a result of the use of the information contained within this document, including, but not limited to, — errors, omissions, or inaccuracies.

Introduction 9

Chapter 1: Making First Impressions 19

Why Are First Impressions Important? 20

How to Radiate Authentic Positivity for a Great First Impression 23

Master the Art of Asking and Answering Questions 38

Summary 41

Chapter 2: Confidence and Mindset 45

How to Build Rock-Solid Confidence 46

How to Boost Confidence 49

Exercises That Help You Eliminate Self-Doubt 53

How to Go from Nervous to Confident in Less Than Two Minutes 56

How to Solidify Confidence and Don't Clam Up in Social Gatherings 60

Positive Thinking and Positive Self-Talk 62

How to Improve Your Self-Image 65

Believe in Your Worth 68

Summary 74

Chapter 3: The Power of Listening and Remembering names For Magnetic Charisma 77

Why You Need Interpersonal Skills to Become Charismatic 78

Learn How to Remember People's Names 85

How to Be a Good Listener 91

Summary 95

Chapter 4: How to Small Talk 99

How to Improve Your Small-Talk Skills 101

How to Lead Conversations to Connect and Spread Your Influence 105

How to Keep Conversations Going to Avoid Awkward Pauses 108

How to Improve Conversation Skills for Memorable Conversations 110

Summary 115

Chapter 5: Storytelling 119

Why You Need to Be a Good Storyteller 120

How to Tell a Convincing Story 123

How to Make Your Story Memorable 130

How to Tell Personal Stories 134

Summary 137

Chapter 6: Presence and Magnetism 141

Strategies for Growing Magnetic Charisma 144

How to Influence People with Your Magnetic Presence 149

How to Speak so That You Command Attention 155

Summary 162

Chapter 7: Being Assertive 163

Develop Social Assertiveness and Get What You Need and Want Out of Interactions 164

Assertiveness Isn't a Personality—It's a Skill 165

How to Start Training to Be Assertive 169

Techniques and Exercises for Assertiveness 180

Summary 187

Chapter 8: Being a Charismatic Leader 191

How to Motivate Others to Be Excited About Doing What You Persuade Them to Do 191

How to Quickly Read Anyone and Know What Triggers Will Influence Them 207

How to Become Influential 208

Summary 215

Chapter 9: Group Interactions 217

Group Interaction Skills for Charismatic Leaders 219

Summary 230

Chapter 10: Handling Conflicts Error! Bookmark not defined.

Types of Conflict and the Best Ways to Find a Solution 236

Why Conflict Occurs? 237

Best Ways to Manage a Conflict 241

Conflict-Solving in Leadership 243

How to Resolve Personal Conflicts to Sway People on Your Side 248

Summary 256

Conclusion Error! Bookmark not defined.

References 269

INTRODUCTION

Do you want to become the best version of yourself? Do you want to become memorable, appeal to people, and find personal and business success? Do you want to overcome shyness and insecurity and become more authentic and popular?

If you want all these things, it means that you

How to be Charismatic & Develop Confidence

have everything it takes to become a charismatic leader, and this book will show you exactly how to do that! How to be Charismatic, Develop Confidence, and Exude Leadership: The Miracle Formula for Magnetic Charisma, Defeating Anxiety, and Winning at Communication will help you get from where you are now to where you want to be by developing ten crucial leadership skills!

This book is for everyone looking to develop social skills, establish deep relationships, open themselves up to the world, and attract people with their bulletproof confidence and intoxicating charisma. Don't believe this can be you? Just wait!

This book will show you the exact techniques and give you the right tools to find the deeply

How to be Charismatic & Develop Confidence

hidden seed of charisma and grow it until it bursts and shines through you in a blinding, jaw-dropping aura that attracts people like moths are drawn to a flame.

How will this book do this for you? It's quite simple. This book will teach you all about charisma and magnetic appeal that you can start nurturing and growing today on any budget just by reaching deep down into the most beautiful depths of your inner being. This book will show you how to find and grab your positive values, strengths, and talents and make them your trademark.

Upon learning how to harvest the fruits of charisma, you'll learn how to develop social skills needed to extend your network of acquaintances, enrich your relationships, upscale your career, and influence people to get what you want. This book will show you how to become an active, engaged, and empathetic listener who makes a killer first impression and leaves people hungry for your presence.

To do this, you will find out how to get people to like you, and it will not be by putting on a mask. No! You will learn how to showcase your authentic self with the way you dress, speak, and shake hands so that everyone who meets you gets to know and love what they see. If you follow the instructions given in this book, you'll be able to show others the genuine, strong, and confident you. You will know how to appeal to people's hidden motivations and desires and connect with what you have in common.

How to be Charismatic & Develop Confidence

Once you learn how to get people to like you, this book will show you how to form better and deeper relationships. You'll learn how to master the art of small talk to set the basis for deeper relationships and leverage these connections to give and take for the sake of mutual progress.

That's right! This book will show you how to become an altruistic, inspiring, and charismatic leader who wears their life's true purpose like one wears a suit and helps other people achieve their goals.

In this book, you will also find out how to become more assertive so that you can balance your feelings and attitude for more productive work and personal relationships. Aren't you tired of being shy and hiding in your cocoon? No more saying yes to things you don't want and doing things that step on your dignity and self-esteem just to please people! In this book, you will learn how to set healthy boundaries so that you can show people what they can and cannot do and what you are and aren't willing to tolerate. More importantly, you'll learn how to do this in a calm, respectful way—that is, respectful both to you and the people around you.

That's right! Assertiveness skills explained in this book will show you how to stand up for yourself without hostility and conflict. Isn't that amazing?

But how do you get there? How do you appeal to people to that extent if you're introverted and shy? What do you do if merely talking to people frightens you? Don't worry—you're covered!

How to be Charismatic & Develop Confidence

This book will give you the basic knowledge for growing and nurturing true confidence and self-esteem based on your authentic personality and best traits. In this book, you'll learn how true confidence looks and how to start practicing it so that you know and understand that you're an infinitely worthy person who can rely on their talents and skills to advance in life. You will learn simple everyday techniques and tips to apply to feel better about yourself and truly believe in your own worth. But that's not all!

This book will tear the misconception that loving yourself means being selfish, and it will show you how to be respectful, truthful, and empathetic. Aside from learning how to become a leader, you will learn how to become a leader who gives and contributes to their group or organization. You will learn how to share ideas and feedback that build everyone up so that you and the people around you are successfully working toward a common goal.

This book will also show you how to use the best of your abilities to observe and read people, as well as use your appearance, performance, and body language to speak and spread your authentic message. Following the principles and instructions given in this book will help you trade the best of your strengths for respect and popularity with your friends, coworkers, and family. Simply put, this book will show you how to reach into the best you have and share it with the world, and then you will receive the sweet fruits of your charismatic labor.

How to be Charismatic & Develop Confidence

Don't wait another minute! Your hidden potentials, core values, and infinite strengths are waiting to be discovered, grown, and plucked to bring you love, acceptance, and success you so deeply desire. With each minute that passes, your potentials are being wasted on self-defeating thoughts and self-sabotaging behaviors, and you are losing time and money on doing things for other people just because you're unable to say no!

Hurry up and start learning to make a great first impression. At the beginning of this book, you'll find out what you can do today so that people remember you and want to connect with you. Aren't you excited to lead?

Get started now!

How to be Charismatic & Develop Confidence

Chapter 1: Making First Impressions

Welcome to your manual for skyrocketing business and personal success by mastering the art of making first impressions. What if I told you that how you come across during the first 30 seconds of meeting new people affects nearly 85 percent of your business success? What if I told you that the person you like takes only a split second to decide whether they like you or not. Doesn't it sound scary? That's because it is! Just imagine. Out of thousands of hours spent learning and doing hard work to build your career, mornings and evenings spent working out to get yourself in shape, all the planning that goes into your career, or all the charity work you do to make the world a better place, those initial 30 seconds determine the majority of your success!

<u>Why Are First Impressions Important?</u>

If you still haven't freaked out, just wait. Remember the last time you made a new acquaintance. Maybe it was a bank clerk, a possible network connection, or your friend's friend who works for a major brand. It could even be your neighbor's coworker, who has a gorgeous son or daughter right about your age.

How to be Charismatic & Develop Confidence

What did these encounters look like? What did you say? How did you look? Were you clean and polished, or were you dressed in rags because you were cleaning your backyard?

How you carry yourself and act around other people determines your success regardless of your true skills, talents, and positive traits. Nailing that first impression can open many doors, point out shortcuts, and help you make long-term connections. But how do you do that? How do you make people remember you and want to talk to you in less than a minute? Lucky for you, you've come to the right place to get your answer.

Right before we get into the strategies for making an awesome first impression, let's briefly address why this is a challenge in the first place. When you're about to meet someone new, your fight-or-flight response gets triggered. Your unconscious brain evaluates whether or not you feel safe around the particular person, and it is particularly keen on detecting anything that's potentially threatening. If you look into the dynamic of first encounters, the truth is that it includes two or more people who instantly start deciding whether the new person seems safe to be around or they're to be avoided. Now, the way this works is that your unconscious mind detects the general appearance, body language, and other peculiarities regarding the other person and makes conclusions based on that. The same goes for those who evaluate you. The best way to make a great first impression is to send out more "green flags" than "red flags."

This means to dress and behave in ways that help people feel safe and eliminate those behaviors that, unconsciously, signal danger.

How to Radiate Authentic Positivity for a Great First Impression

Having a positive attitude means allowing the best of you to shine through your attitude and conversations. However, this positivity needs to be genuine and not imposed (i.e., toxic positivity). It's important to remember to consistently work on how you see the world so that you're able to maintain a positive, optimistic outlook on a situation while acknowledging the present reality. A general rule might be that people prefer positive people. However, if your job is to market yourself as a grief consultant, to say that you should act punchy and upbeat would be wrong. In this situation, you should level your mindset to be empathetic with the people you talk to, but be positive-oriented in the way you send your messages and talk to them. When talking to people in a business setting or at a party, it would be appropriate to show your most confident, upbeat self. What do you do when that's inappropriate? Then you adjust to how you can make the situation better.

Toxic positivity, on the other hand, is present in people we perceive as disingenuous. These people make false claims and statements of not only their success but also what others can do. Their intentions are self-involved, and that's easy to notice. They can only fool those who are emotionally and mentally vulnerable—and even that is only temporary. So when speaking about positivity, keep in mind that I'm referring to a genuinely helpful, optimistic attitude in your appearance and mannerisms aimed at making everyone around you feel a bit better than they felt before they met you. At times, you will do this using jokes, and other times, it will be through consolation and the words of support.

7 Steps to Radiate positivity:

1. Stay in the moment.

To display this quality, make sure to leave all stresses and disruptions at home, and be focused entirely on the situation and people present. At the same time, learn not to allow other people to take away your cool. A lot of the time, it's impossible to shelter yourself from the influence of those we'd call "toxic" people. When you find yourself in a situation where the first impression matters, try not to react to other people's toxic or provocative behavior. If your reaction can't help or bring any kind of improvement, there's no reason to respond at all.

2. Tweak your appearance.

Whether we like it or not, we're all judged by first impressions. The way you come across the first couple of minutes may affect whether or not you'll get a job, a promotion, a date, a client, and so many other things. We're all taught we shouldn't care what people think about us, and it's indeed healthier not to obsess over it. However, it's essential to understand how the first couple of seconds may affect how others see you based on things like your facial expression, body language, clothes, and mannerisms. People around you evaluate your personality based on what they see on the surface. However, how will tweaking your appearance help make a great first impression? There are a couple of things you can do to present yourself in an authentic, genuine, and respectful manner.

Showcase respect. Want people to respect you? Start displaying respect first by being considerate of other people and their time. Particularly, be punctual and accountable. Whenever you're meeting someone new, make sure to arrive either early or on time. If you're late on your first appointment, you can expect to leave a bad first impression.

How to be Charismatic & Develop Confidence

Mind your personal representation. Make sure that the way you dress for the occasion gives off the impression you want to create. Ideally, your outfit should be suitable for the situation. It needs to be a reflection of your unique, authentic personality and strategically chosen to send subtle cues and messages. Your outfit doesn't have to be a luxurious one, and you don't always have to be dressed elegantly to make the right impression. A suitable outfit will leave a memorable impression, and what better way to do that than showing up your unique, amazing style? However, it's important that you're clean and dressed appropriately, whether you're at work or in a networking event. In this sense, it's important to note that different occasions will require different outfits.

You wouldn't go to a wedding party in the same

outfit you'd go to a business meeting. However, there are also many classic, timeless, chic outfits that, believe it or not, suit multiple different occasions. For example, the "little black dress" is a uniform design that you can wear in different situations from work to a wedding, depending on how you use accessories and style the outfit. For men, simple elegance, like plain black pants and blazer with a white or any neutral-color shirt, is also universally acceptable for the majority of different settings. If you're on a budget, think about getting a couple of new classic chic items you can wear throughout the entire day and still leave a great impression no matter where you show up.

Be authentic. Discovering your authenticity and unique behaviors helps you fit into any environment but still stay loyal to yourself. To be charismatic, you have to fit in at least a little bit. You're looking to belong but still stand out. Belonging, of course, stems from having certain connections to the group or a situation, whether it's a mutual goal or a problem to solve. Being your authentic self means having respect and integrity. It means respecting the integrity of the people you meet the same way you respect yourself. This will help you build up confidence and expand your social network.

3. Put on a smile.

Smiling and being in a good mood is memorable, and people always love being around those people who are cheerful and upbeat. A smile radiates warmth and confidence that will make people around you feel good as well. However, make sure not to smile too much and artificially. It could come across as insecure, fake, and creepy and give people the wrong idea about you.

4. Show confidence.

Confidence is one of the most attractive human qualities. It speaks more about you than can be said in your résumé. Showing confidence through your body language, eye contact, smile, and handshake makes people around you feel secure. While it's common for people to feel insecure when meeting other people, if your nervousness makes you uncomfortable and takes away from your experience, you can take some time before the meeting and work through your nervousness and anxiety. Another great way to appear confident when you're meeting someone for the first time is to set time aside to get appropriately ready, have everything you need in order, get there on time, and have a couple of minutes to spare to take a couple of deep breaths and calm down.

There's another way to cope with this kind of nervousness, and it is to accept it and be genuinely comfortable with it. Many people joke about their awkwardness and social mishaps, which help everyone feel more comfortable. There's nothing wrong with being shy. If you are shy, what you should aim for is to stop that shyness from keeping you from connecting with people.

5. Practice small talk.

Usually, during small talk, people exchange

seemingly superficial questions and answers. Small talk may sound irrelevant, but it most certainly isn't. There are many subtleties we reveal about our personalities through small talk, and it is an excellent opportunity to connect with a person and take the conversation in a more significant direction. Every verbal exchange is a dynamic of giving and receiving information.

6. Grow your emotional intelligence.

What better way to master first impressions than to study emotional intelligence? You might think that your talents, qualities, and work results speak for themselves, but the reality couldn't be more different. People subconsciously make far more conclusions than one would care to admit. If you want to

How to be Charismatic & Develop Confidence

leave a good first impression, you should develop emotional intelligence skills to detect, interpret, and respond appropriately to your own and other people's feelings. These skills have developed remarkable communication abilities that help solve conflicts, negotiate, and work toward the common goal in almost every setting. People who notice that you possess sharp emotional intelligence will think of you as dependable and reliable.

But what is emotional intelligence? As the name suggests, it is the ability to be intelligent about feelings. More precisely, it means to have skills to look through superficial behaviors and detect people's feelings and intentions. To develop these skills, you first need to develop your own emotional awareness, which is the ability to understand how you truly feel. More importantly, developing emotional intelligence helps you see how your emotions guide and affect your motivations, decisions, and behavior. There are a couple of ways to nurture your emotional intelligence.

Practice self-reflection. Self-reflection is a method through which you evaluate how you think and feel and, more importantly, how that affects your actions. Before showing up to your meeting, take a moment or two to reflect on what you think and how you feel in these situations. This will help you match your attitude to the person you're speaking to or a situation you're in. If you're nervous and anxious, it's possible for your mindset to be inward-focused, and you lose the connection with the dynamic of the situation.

How to be Charismatic & Develop Confidence

Level your energy. Learning how to adjust your energy to the situation and the person you talk to helps you connect and relate to them. With your emotional intelligence skills well developed, you will be able to adjust your body language and energy to the room. For example, a formal setting and a wedding party will require two different approaches to how you carry yourself.

Focus on the other person. Paying attention to what the other person is talking about and being a careful listener helps you connect and leave an impression. For this, it is also vital to remove any distractions and put away your phone to maintain natural, steady eye contact. To avoid coming across as uninterested, you shouldn't interrupt another person while they're speaking. Also, if you talk to another person while thinking about the next thing you're about to say, it can come across as rude and uninterested as well.

7. Focus on common interests.

Finding something that helps you relate to the person you're talking to helps find interesting topics for both of you to enjoy. This way, the other person will remember that they related to you in some way, particularly if the topic was fun and interesting. One of the best ways to find common interests with another person is to ask questions. However, pay attention not to come across as an interrogator. If another person is shy, they might feel uncomfortable being consistently asked questions.

Master the Art of Asking and Answering Questions

Common courtesy is to begin a conversation by asking some basic questions about the other person. Typically, in informal settings like meeting and job interviews, those higher on the ladder will initiate the conversation and ask questions, while the ones aiming to get a job or raise funds for their business will be the ones answering them. When answering common questions, it's important to remember to keep your answers medium length and open-ended. What does this mean?

You should never give one-word answers unless specifically told to do so. Answering questions like "Where you are from?" and "What do you do?" can be tricky for shy people, as they might give one-word answers and freeze the conversation. Instead, you should provide answers that say a little bit more about you and comment on what you like and appreciate about where you're from and what you do. You can also give a backstory of how you started working on a job you're currently at.

Aside from these common questions, questions that revolve around your work and career are quite common in job interviews and networking events. Here's how to answer some of the specific questions during job interviews:

"Why do you think you're the right person?" Whichever position you're applying for, the interviewer will want to know what drives you and makes you excited to do the job. Here, you should take the opportunity to speak about

skills and experiences and how you can use them to contribute to the organization in that particular position.

"Why are you changing jobs?" Interviewers will want to know which circumstances led you to quit the current job and look for another one. They will want to know all about your past work record and employment history, as well as why you left your previous job. It's imperative to give well-thought-out but genuine answers, or else you might leave a bad first impression.

You, too, have the right to ask questions during interviews. Here, you can take the opportunity to find out more about the job post they advertised. Asking questions about details that are important to you shows initiative, and it shows that you're interested in the entire organization and not just getting a job.

Ask about leadership and career development. Whether or not it will be appropriate to ask this question during a job interview depends on many factors, mainly on the work culture of the company. If you notice that the company values personal goals and leadership development, you can share your goals and find out how the position relates to your idea of personal growth. If you don't think this approach is right for the position you're applying for, you can show interest in senior management or other team members and ask how they obtained their positions and how long have they been with the company.

Summary

In this chapter, you learned that first

How to be Charismatic & Develop Confidence

impressions can make or break your chances of success all around. You learned that to make a great first impression, you must:

- Be considerate, present in the moment, and focused on the people around you
- Look and act confident, which you'll show with a proud, strong, tall posture
- Master the art of casual conversation
- Focus on talking about mutual-interest topics and goals
- Ask and answer open-ended questions that are interesting, strategic, appropriate, and engaging.

Now that you know how to make a great first impression, it's time to learn how to build and exude true confidence. In the next chapter, you'll find out not only how to look and act but

How to be Charismatic & Develop Confidence

also how to nurture the rock-solid confidence of a true leader.

How to be Charismatic & Develop Confidence

CHAPTER 2: CONFIDENCE AND MINDSET

Confident people are universally attractive. They are easy to work with, trustworthy, and inspiring for others. Their inviting attitude attracts people around them. However, it's not always easy to remain confident in your abilities. This can be particularly difficult for those who are self-critical or those in an environment where other people put them down. Luckily, there are many things you can do to improve your self-confidence.

How to Build Rock-Solid Confidence

Self-confident people are able to trust their abilities and judgment and feel worthy while embracing their imperfections. They understand that no one is perfect. They're not chasing after perfectionism; instead, they accept their limitations as something natural and normal. Being self-confident also relates to self-efficacy, which is the ability to feel like we're competent to achieve goals and gain skills. This feeling helps up open up to the idea that we're able to do things if we put in enough effort, accounting for realistic obstacles and chances of failure.

Self-esteem, on the other hand, is a feeling or

How to be Charismatic & Develop Confidence

an acknowledgment that we have the right to be happy and appreciate ourselves regardless of what goes on in our lives. When people condition their self-esteem with exterior validation and proof of success, that means that they only allow themselves to feel good when the conditions for that are in place. Whenever a challenge arises, they start feeling bad about themselves and deny their right to happiness. As you can see, this isn't a great way to deal with challenges, isn't it? When you're making first impressions, people tend to notice these things about a person's character. It can cause mistrust in people, as they sense a person will lose their grip in situations that are stressful and challenging, which is not something most people want at work or in personal life.

A sense of self-esteem also links to caring too

much about whether or not people around us approve what we do. While we're in very little control of whether or not someone will approve our actions, learning how to process criticism and rejection is valuable here (Klitch & Feldman, 1992). Low self-esteem may cause you to take negative feedback of any kind too personally and feel like it speaks about your personality when, in fact, it only reflects your actions.

As you can see, as opposed to a strong, confident appearance that instills trust, acting insecure and shy can make people see you as someone they don't necessarily want on their team or in their life, particularly if they were already hurt by someone else's insecurity. You may not be aware of this, but people who are led by their insecurities tend to make many mistakes at work and in personal relationships that can harm others (Griffin et al., 2007).

Actions that serve to save face or cover an error can make people feel invisible and insignificant. The same is true when you are too shy to express feelings and show another person you value them being in your life. On the surface, people call those who are insecure or shy, harmless and pleasant, while they unconsciously perceive them as a potential liability. At the very least, people don't tend to remember those who are timid and withdrawn.

How to Boost Confidence

Most people think that strengthening one's confidence means eliminating insecurities. You might think that if you simply address those issues that make you feel insecure, you will automatically become confident. While

How to be Charismatic & Develop Confidence

confronting personal fears and limitations does help reduce the impact of low confidence on your life, it doesn't heal the inner wound completely. The missing link in growing your self-esteem is the habit of strengthening it, much like the empathy muscle mentioned earlier.

Here are a couple of ways to develop confidence and self-esteem:

1. Face and challenge negative thoughts. Think about the reasons why you feel so bad about yourself, and find out which positive thoughts and ideas outweigh those negatives.

2. Practice healthy self-care. Feeling and looking bad won't help you feel more confident. To enhance your well-being, embrace diet improvements and exercise. Living a healthy lifestyle helps reduce stress and makes you feel better about yourself. Aside from exercising, setting aside enough time to relax each day also helps you reduce stress and tension.

3. *Be goal-oriented.* Take some time each day to think through your life goals. Think about the things you can achieve and write down your thoughts. Track your accomplishments as you complete goals, keep yourself motivated, and collect the evidence that will strengthen your confidence and self-esteem. Oftentimes, people with low self-esteem notice their failures but not their successes. For example, they stress more about the fact that they can't find a job in their field with a college degree instead of focusing on how proud they are for earning their degree and working another job until a better opportunity arises. By collecting evidence of your accomplishments, you'll focus more on the good things you've done instead of those you think prove your failure or lack of worth.

4. Step out of your head. There's nothing more nurturing for one's self-esteem as practicing love, care, and empathy for others. Research shows that there are actually health benefits or so-called "happy highs" in people who do charitable work (Deiner & Seligman, 2002). When you step out of your mental prison, where your thought process revolves around plans, ambitions, and insecurities, and forget about them for a little bit to help others, your brain switches to feeling happy and proud for having helped or cared for others around you.

Exercises That Help You Eliminate Self-Doubt

Do you doubt yourself when you're nervous or fear you'll say something wrong? Here are a couple of proven strategies to not allow self-doubt to get to you:

1. *Stop negative thoughts.* Never allow discouraging thoughts to spiral out of control. Understand that shyness and insecurity are natural and normal and that everyone experiences thoughts of insecurity. These thoughts have a physiological background, and you can't eliminate them. But you can stop yourself when you notice you're focusing on them and giving them too much of your time. When you're about to meet someone new, and you start thinking negative thoughts about yourself, just say "Stop."

2. Bring back encouraging memories. Be it the first time you successfully rode a bike or you jumped off a tall wall thinking your life is about to end only to land safely and without a scratch, recalling encouraging memories helps you remind yourself of your ability to succeed and overcome obstacles. Encouraging memories and experiences have the power to instantly relieve anxiety and bring back the smile on your face, making it easier to give a confident handshake and share eye contact that's reassuring for both you and the other person.

3. Get feedback. One of the great ways to overcome insecurity is to get frequent, unbiased feedback. It will help you be more aware of your strengths compared to weaknesses. Talking about your insecurities with friends and family will undoubtedly result in reassurance in how valuable you are to them, which will have a long-term empowering effect.

4. *Stop comparing yourself to others.* There is a correct way to estimate the quality and efficiency of your work, but comparing yourself to others isn't one of them. It's because you're comparing yourself against an exaggerated impression of how another person's life looks. You might admire someone's looks and career, but you don't know how much effort they put into these areas and whether or not they may lack some of the things you have.

5. *Write a journal.* We tend to forget positives and focus on negatives. It is a habit that's hard to shake for a 21st-century human. Mainly, this is because we are so hard on ourselves and aim for perfectionist goals. Create a habit of writing down at least one page in your journal each day, summing up at least three things you're proud of and three things you want to do differently in the future.

And that's it! These strategies will undoubtedly help you overcome that inherent insecurity and let your best self shine through.

How to Go from Nervous to Confident in Less Than Two Minutes

Building true confidence is a long-term venture. It's safe to say that, while you should be patient with improving your self-image and learning how to believe in your strength for months and years, you're going to need quick, effective strategies to act confidently in the meantime. Here's how to boost your confidence instantly for a killer first impression:

1. Stand tall. Straighten your back, keep your chin up, and pull your shoulders back. Make sure your hands are still. Your posture should be straight, chest open, with your head slightly tilted back. This way, you will open up your posture for communication and appear more approachable. As you start to look more confident, people will find it more interesting to interact with you.

2. Create new experiences. If your routines are constant and predictable, make sure to check out some new restaurants and coffee shops, or perhaps try out a new sport, or have a fun trip. New experiences help you change your environment a bit, which inspires creativity and appreciation of the things around you.

3. *Focus on your talents.* Doing new things does challenge your fears and boosts confidence, but doing something you're good at strengthens your belief in yourself. Working on your talents and engaging in hobbies help you see what you're capable of. This enforces a positive self-image and enables you to think highly about yourself.

4. *Change perspective.* Questioning whether situations and events are truly as bad as they seem helps you question negative thinking patterns and overcome them gradually. Whenever you feel like you're failing or like you've embarrassed yourself, try to challenge these thoughts by asking yourself:

- "Is there a way to turn the situation around so that it works in your favor?"
- "Are there any hidden benefits to the situation you can focus on?"
- "Is there a better way to look at the situation?"
- "What lesson can I learn from this that will help me in the future?"

5. Focus on your breathing. Whenever you start feeling shy and insecure, your heart rate will increase, and your breathing will become shallow. Now, you're low on oxygen, which will only increase your anxiety. Instead, focus on taking three to five deep and even breaths. This will help you calm down and have more positive thoughts about yourself.

How to Solidify Confidence and Don't Clam Up in Social Gatherings

As you learn how to build rock-solid confidence, you shouldn't let shyness prevent you from attending and enjoying social gatherings. If you're shy or socially anxious, there are a couple of techniques you can use to feel more socially competent and be more present during social events.

Here are a couple of tips to be more confident during social events:

1. Get ready. Being self-conscious will ruin your mood, and one of the ways to prevent it is to be prepared. Make a list of what you want to do to get ready for your workday, a trip with friends, a party, or a meeting. Write down what your main purpose is, what you want to say and do, and, more importantly, how you'll plan your look. Think about what you'll wear and how to do your hairstyle. What are the self-maintenance items to cross off (e.g., shaving, getting a haircut, or visiting a cosmetician)? Feeling like you're all ready and polished will boost your confidence.

2. *Focus outwards.* Instead of focusing on what you think and how you feel, look at the room and notice a couple of things you like. Pay attention to the drinks and food, and think about the snacks you'd like to try out. Also, try observing other people. How do they look? What are they doing? What are their roles? What do you like about them? Thoughts like these help you stay focused on the exterior and forget about nervousness, at least temporarily.

3. *Keep yourself busy.* Being active, talking to other people, and smiling will help pass the time and feel better. The more you engage with other people, the more you'll forget about negative and anxious thoughts. If you ever start to feel anxious thoughts arising, shift your attention to other people, and ask more questions about them. This will make for a pleasant chat and help you overcome anxiety.

Positive Thinking and Positive Self-Talk

Positive self-talk can help you increase not only your performance but also how you feel about yourself overall. A negative self-image can sabotage all areas of life, from health to relationships and even work. On the other hand, a positive self-image can help you boost your shape, advance career, and introduce the right people into your life.

Positive self-talk serves to change your thinking patterns gradually and consciously. It revolves around catching yourself making an inaccurate, exaggerated negative statement or thought about yourself and examining and changing it. Here's how you can apply positive self-talk to improve confidence and boost self-image (Neck & Manz, 1992):

1. *Identify negative self-talk.* Conscious negative thoughts are easy to spot, but unconscious negative thoughts work differently. You don't register them, but they suddenly make you feel tense or afraid without any reason. More importantly, they reduce your drive and motivation. Whenever you suddenly feel down or you observe that you're now having self-defeating thoughts, analyze them. Ask yourself whether these thoughts are accurate or there's a chance they aren't.

2. Reframe negative self-talk. Once you've discovered a self-defeating thought pattern, try to tell a different story to yourself. Reword the same statements in a way that's positive, optimistic, and respectful of your personality. If you find it difficult, try reframing negative statements to make them more realistic. This eliminates negative exaggerations, which occur once catastrophic thinking skews your judgement.

3. Practice positive self-talk. Develop a routine of saying positive affirmations about yourself each day. These affirmations should be believable, or else they might trigger anxiety.

How to Improve Your Self-Image

What exactly can you do to improve your self-image? First things first—you need to identify your negative thoughts and review the reasons why you have a negative self-image.

Negative self-image manifests itself in four different self-sabotaging behaviors. First, it makes you personalize negative experiences and blame yourself for everything that goes wrong in your life. Second, this negative perspective gets unrealistically magnified. You're capable of ignoring all the positive aspects of a situation, and instead, focus only on the negatives. This thought process becomes habitual and unconscious, creating a self-sabotaging pattern that makes you look at yourself in a negative light. Third, you start expecting the worst. The more you focus on the negatives, the worse outcomes you start to expect, even if the catastrophic scenario opposes logic. Fourth, you start thinking in polarizing ways. Situations are either black or white without the possibility that there are positives in negative situations and other ways around.

Once you start recognizing your negative thinking patterns, you can move on to use the following strategies to improve your self-image gradually (Mayo et al., 2012):

1. *Battle negative self-talk.* Learning how to identify the negative things you think about yourself will help you start opposing them with rational evidence. Looking into what scares you the most about interactions will help you rationalize whether or not the scenario is realistic, and it will prepare you for the best possible outcome. As you mingle around and socialize, pay attention to when negative self-talk starts to arise. As soon as this happens, let yourself know that you are wrong and oppose these thoughts with realistic yet more optimistic ones.

2. *Take yourself less seriously.* Negative self-image sometimes manifests itself in some strange behaviors. Perhaps you exaggerate in your mind how serious a meeting will be and get ready to give a detailed presentation only to realize everyone else just came there to share a couple of important points and order a pizza. Try to see the humor in your negative experiences. Over time, this will help you dread catastrophic outcomes less.

3. *Tune into positivity.* People with negative self-image don't benefit from melancholic content. Choosing to watch, read, and listen to positive content may be the best solution in the long run (Berry & Hansen, 1996). Look around and discover the items, choices, and other influences in your life that spark negative feelings. You may like watching horror movies, but if you tend to become upset easily, perhaps you should choose a comedy over watching *Annabelle* tonight. Moreover, try wearing light-colored clothes instead of dark ones, or play some calming ambiance music instead of gothic rock.

Believe in Your Worth

Having a high sense of self-worth means having

How to be Charismatic & Develop Confidence

a profoundly positive opinion of yourself and carrying unshakable faith in your abilities. The challenging part here is that this faith needs to persist through challenges and endure whenever you fail. People who have a high level of self-worth feel like they deserve love, happiness, success, money, and all the wonderful things in life. Do you truly feel like that? Many of us are raised to think that we should have all these things, but we don't necessarily feel like we deserve them. This is the reason why we're plagued by anxiety, fear of failure, and many other self-imposed limitations that diminish confidence and productivity. How do we change this?

The answer is by making consistent, daily efforts to feel and think good about ourselves. Now, this is easier said than done. Luckily for you, there are many easy, reasonable steps you can take each day to nurture your sense of self-worth:

Step 1: Detect and identify how you think and feel about yourself. You can do this by thinking about or visualizing who you are when you take away all attachments to your physical life. This means imagining yourself without connections, possessions, accomplishments, and other material things. When you see yourself all alone, with nothing holding you back, what is it that's left? How would you feel knowing that all you have left is yourself? What do you possess that would be of real value? This is the part where you discover what you genuinely like and admire about yourself.

Step 2: Accept who you are. Most of us go by

an ideal image of ourselves that doesn't always represent our true, authentic skills, desires, passions, and abilities. Now that you've discovered who you think you are and how you feel about yourself, it's time to accept it. There's a possibility you don't particularly appreciate what you've discovered. Perhaps you think your qualities are not enough. So what? The very act of acceptance means starting to feel and think positively about what you've discovered yourself to be. Even if your level of self-worth isn't at the desired level, still accept it and remember that from now on, you can only improve. The trick with acceptance is to push that deep, unconscious button and say, "This is it, and this is enough. I am enough." Just doing this will kickstart a chain of unconscious processes that will shift your mindset. Here, it's essential to understand that you're accepting yourself with all the positive and negative qualities because you have the right to have negative traits too. Everyone is at least a bit selfish, envious, lazy, or mean at times. That doesn't make you a bad person.

Step 3: *Start loving yourself.* Nurturing self-love needs to be done every single day and particularly when you feel like you're failing. You always, under all conditions, have the right to feel compassionate, generous, kind, and patient with yourself. But don't confuse this with accepting and condoning doing negative things. Many people deny love to themselves, thinking that if they accept and love their whole being unconditionally, they'll unleash some sort of selfish, destructive inner monster. That's not true. Quite the opposite, now that you're giving yourself unconditional and endless love, you will feel more aware of other people's needs and have abundant supplies of tolerance and generosity for everyone else. To nurture true self-love, don't forget to repeat encouraging mantras like "I love and value myself," "I accept and love myself unconditionally," and "I believe in my worth and competence."

After you've done this, it's time to start recognizing that you don't have to please others. Review and look into all the things you do just to fulfill other people's expectations. Many people feel that it is selfish not to please others, but it's not. Instead, you'll enter a stage of self-responsibility, where you realize that you and you alone are solely responsible for your life and well-being.

How to be Charismatic & Develop Confidence

Summary

In this chapter, you learned that charisma, networking, and influence require building strong confidence, unshakeable self-esteem, and positive self-image.

To grow strong self-confidence, you have to challenge negative thoughts, practice healthy self-care, stay focused on your goals, and be in the present moment.

To eliminate self-doubt, you need to stop negative thoughts, recall positive experiences, ask for feedback on your actions and performance, stop comparing yourself to others, and keep track of your thoughts and experiences by journaling.

To boost confidence instantly, stand straight

How to be Charismatic & Develop Confidence

and tall, meet different people and create new experiences, concentrate on your talents, change your perspective, and focus on your breathing to calm down and regain mental clarity.

Chapter 3: The Power of Listening and Remembering Names for Magnetic Charisma

A person's name is to him or her the sweetest and most important sound in any language.

—Dale Carnegie

Becoming charismatic starts with learning how to connect with other people. Charisma is a complex set of qualities that make a person attractive. It is an invisible quality that stems from one's inner traits rather than the exterior. Charisma is also an essential trait of all public figures or leaders, whether they're politicians, professors, or actors. It also revolves around the power of persuasion—the ability to motivate people into doing what you want. It is practiced using one's words, facial expressions, and body language. A charismatic appeal motivates and inspires others, so they become attached to the person they find inspiring. However, it's not a skill taught openly or directly. But how can you become more charismatic?

Why You Need Interpersonal Skills to Become Charismatic

The first step in becoming a charismatic leader is to develop your interpersonal or

How to be Charismatic & Develop Confidence

communication skills. These skills, while inborn, can be grown and developed. Personal charisma revolves around being genuinely interested in people and detaching from devices and inner negativity that might be present while you converse.

Another important yet intangible element of charisma is the art of influencing people to like you. But how do you do this when you're not able to affect what others think? The answer is by exploring and showcasing the utmost best of your personality and traits. When natural and authentic, charisma can last through years and even decades. When forced and inauthentic, it can become drained. To become truly charismatic, you'll have to exercise confidence skills and master the art of likeability, listening, and body language.

How to be Charismatic & Develop Confidence

The five basic skills needed to become charismatic include authenticity, rapport building, listening skills, and confidence. In this chapter, we'll focus on those skills you need so that you can create deeper connections with people you talk to. Growing these skills will help you connect with an entire group of people. This happens as the charisma shines in your appearance—from your eyes to your body language:

1. *Correct your posture.* First, pay attention to your posture. Sit and stand straight with your chest open to display inner strength and openness. The two relate because people become closed, which they display by slouching when they feel weak. This means you need to keep an open body posture, which will make you more approachable. Also, make sure to pay attention to other people's body language. It shows who feels secure, confident, inviting and who needs empathy and encouragement.

2. Respect other people's personal space. Another important part of connecting with people is to respect other people's personal space. Make sure never to get too close or touch people while you're talking if you don't know them well. When talking to other people, try finding common ground even if your opinions don't agree. One of the great ways to show disagreement is to express your argument and then state that you can see how and why certain situations or events could lead the person to think and feel the way they do. Using open-ended questions keeps the conversation going and helps you move through different topics to learn more about the other person. You build rapport by matching facial expressions and body language to the other person and mentioning their name multiple times throughout a conversation.

3. *Have a sense of humor.* Being fun and likable is also a big part of nurturing connectivity. However, humor needs to be authentic to your personality and suitable to the occasion. One of the great ways to develop a natural, unique sense of humor is to study the style of comedians you like the most and then think about how you can implement their style into your daily conversations.

4. *Be considerate and empathetic.* Empathy is an amazing ability to put yourself into the shoes of the other person and understand how they think and feel. In the majority of situations, I'd say that people tend to be impressed by those who show care and consideration and turned off by those who are overly self-involved. But how do you make this distinction when your goal is to showcase your personality or skills? This is a great thought-provoker because it could help you solve many internal conflicts around how and why being successful doesn't mean that others have to fail. Connecting with other people by paying attention to their needs doesn't take away the focus from you. Quite the opposite, you become the center of attention because now the other person sees you as someone who understands them. This, too, needs to be genuine because people are good at noticing those who pretend to be helpful only to try and manipulate. The people you meet as you climb up the career ladder will distinguish a genuine attitude from a fake one. There are many great ways to practice empathy because it isn't only a feeling. Empathy is a mental and emotional ability, a muscle you can train the same way you can train your abs.

From empathy, you gain a better understanding of mutual goals, more functional communication, and easier conflict solving. Many other valuable skills arise from simply seeing through people's defense mechanisms. Say you apply for a job, and the interviewer notices that you are considerate and empathetic. What does that tell them? It shows that you can understand work dynamics and other people's direct and hidden intentions. The moment your coworkers realize that, they'll know they can trust you with more demanding work tasks, as you can balance the workflow

How to be Charismatic & Develop Confidence

and prevent toxicity or conflicts from arising in a workgroup.

Now that you know the skills you need to "break the ice," you can make people feel more comfortable and open up more easily, which is essential in becoming a charismatic leader.

Learn How to Remember People's Names

Not everyone is good at remembering names, but there are times in your life when it's necessary. Sometimes forgetting someone's name can even become a problem. For example, introducing yourself and your coworkers to other people can go awkward if, let's say, you can't remember the names of the people you're with. A part of being charismatic

How to be Charismatic & Develop Confidence

(and a quite important one) is to make the people around you feel important. The first way to do it is, for starters, to know their names.

If you have trouble remembering people's names, you should work on it because having someone forget their name can make people around you feel unimportant. Knowing someone's name, on the other hand, is one of the essential persuasion tools. Addressing a person by their name makes the conversation more personal, and it helps people to open up to hearing your ideas.

Now, let's say that you're someone who has trouble remembering names. If you want to change that, the first thing you need to know is why you have this problem in the first place. Our unconscious minds trigger "danger signals"

How to be Charismatic & Develop Confidence

each time we're in an unfamiliar situation. While people who are just introducing themselves might look completely comfortable and confident, their unconscious minds are anxious and, in fact, afraid (Cohen, 1990).

Nowadays, we love getting to know new people, and it's almost always a good, positive situation in our lives. But for our ancient ancestors, this was a potentially dangerous situation. In 2020, we get to know people because we want to bond with them, while some 20,000 years back in history, a primal human would have an entire ritual of exchanging different signs and behaviors to determine whether the other primate is a friend or a foe (Cohen, 1990). We skip through that whole process and move straight into handshakes, so the names said along the way slip by us. When you forget people's names, it simply means that you experience a momentary "stranger danger" physiological reaction, but there are some things you can do to change this.

Another reason why remembering names can be challenging is that our brains are primarily focused on remembering faces. If you think about it, when you meet another person, you're mainly focused on figuring out or noticing their face and other important information (e.g., age, gender, and their place in the hierarchy of the group).

That being said, the answer to how you can start remembering people's names is a quite simple one: focus on it. When you're introducing yourself to new people, make a conscious effort to listen, remember, and repeat their name. That, of course, can be done in quite natural ways that spark conversations. For example, after another person tells you their name, and let's say you're still shaking hands, introduce a question like, "Hi, [name], how are you doing?" or "Nice to meet you, [name]."

During the first couple of minutes of conversation, try repeating the name once or twice—not too much, though, because it might come across as strange. Another way to remember people's names, of course, when the situation is appropriate is to ask a person to spell their name out or use a mnemonic device. The first is appropriate when the conversation isn't very casual. It's also suitable when you're writing down information, filling out forms, or having some other type of formal interaction where another person is providing their info.

When you have people's names written down, you can use a mnemonic device, which is a technique with which you associate a person's name to another similar or memorable word or phrase. Another way to make remembering people's names easier is to associate them with other familiar people, faces, and objects. Say you meet a woman named Jasmine. What better way to remember it than by visualizing the flower itself?

Simply committing to making an effort to remember people's names usually helps focus on it more. The main reason why you have issues remembering names is that your mind goes somewhere else during introductions. Putting a conscious effort into staying in the present moment helps.

How to Be a Good Listener

Charismatic people are devoted to listening to others, which makes people around them feel understood. Being a good listener is the next most important trait of a charismatic leader. It conveys interest into what another person is talking about, signaling that you value them and the things they're trying to say.

If you don't think of yourself as a prime listener out there, the fault is not entirely on you, and it doesn't mean you're egocentric or self-involved. A lot of the time (and particularly when we're busy or stressed), we're more focused on our own issues and find it more difficult to focus on what the people around us are talking about. Luckily, there are many great

How to be Charismatic & Develop Confidence

ways for you to gain great listening skills:

1. Be present in the moment. Don't let your mind wander off in different directions, but decide to stay focused on the conversation. The effort counts here because staying focused will take some time to learn, particularly if you're stressed and in a hurry. Either way, make sure to maintain eye contact with the person who is talking, and by all means, avoid looking out the window or looking at your phone.

2. Summarize their message. The best way to make a person feel heard is to sum up what they just said, making sure you got everything right. This is also good to avoid miscommunications.

3. Don't interrupt. Wait patiently until another person is finished talking before you start talking. Interrupting is a spontaneous habit, and the more you practice, the more you encourage it. However, the more you stop yourself when you're about to interrupt, the easier it will get over time. If you must interrupt someone to take a call or because you're in a rush, make sure to apologize before saying what you're about to say.

4. Listen with your eyes and face. Eye contact and facial expressions can tell whether or not you're listening, and it shows how you feel and what you think while the other person is talking. While you don't have to maintain constant eye contact, aim to maximize it, and then break it naturally when you're trying to process or visualize what the other person is talking about. When it comes to facial expressions, attune them to the occasion and the emotion of the conversation. A natural way to do this is by empathizing with another person, which is particularly healthy if you have trouble controlling anxious thoughts.

5. Incorporate head movements. Nodding and tilting your head are great ways to show that you're listening. These movements should flow naturally through the conversation. They are a sign that you are processing and understanding what another person is saying.

6. Move your body. You can slightly tilt toward the person, which shows your focus on their story. However, use this movement cautiously as you don't want to intrude on another person's private space. This movement is appropriate when you're sitting. Another important tip is to point your entire body, head to toe, to the person you're talking to. If you're in a group, make sure to turn your body toward the group.

7. Give affirming remarks. Phrases like "I see," "That's great," "I understand," and others are important to remain an active participant in the conversation and not just a passive listener.

8. Ask questions. Asking questions in a conversation shows your interest in the topic and what the other person is trying to say. However, it's crucial that these questions are natural and logical. They should reflect a genuine interest in the answer.

Summary

In this chapter, you learned how to harvest the fruits of careful listening to get people to open up and trust you and, ultimately, remember you. You'll need listening skills to advance in all areas of life, including leadership. You learned that to become an active listener, you need to do the following:

- Develop listening skills by staying present in the moment of conversation. Focus on what the other person is saying and show interest in their words.
- Remember people's names. To truly engage and leave a good impression, you can't afford to forget people's names. Remembering names is made easier by repeating a person's name multiple times during a conversation and using associations and mnemonic tools to recall the names that are hard to retain in your memory.

How to be Charismatic & Develop Confidence

- Be a good listener. Listening isn't just absorbing other people's words; it is also about making them feel like they're being heard. For this, you have to listen more than speak. Mimic another person's body language. Move your head to show that you're paying attention. Summarize their words. Ask questions and give answers.

How to be Charismatic & Develop Confidence

Chapter 4: How to Small Talk

In leadership, small talk is an integral part of networking. It helps you make positive first impressions and become an influential leader. More importantly, it requires and boosts social skills. Introverts may not enjoy this part of networking, but it helps build rapport and connect with new customers, peers, and coworkers to climb to the top. When discussing making small talk in leadership, it's important to remember that how you feel on the inside shines through your appearance. The very anticipation of awkwardness can very well create tension and anxiety, so learning how to overcome it is crucial for good networking.

When thinking about exceptional small talk, it's important not to bother yourself with what you'll say or do, anticipating to say something unintelligent or embarrassing yourself. While you should have your conversations planned out, you shouldn't entirely focus on this part of the process. Aside from this, be authentic and avoid asking common lazy questions people hear about most of the time they meet someone new. At least you shouldn't start a conversation like that. Instead, start with something unique and original, perhaps by complimenting a person's outfit or saying something funny about the venue. For example, you can ask a person more profound questions about their career choice (e.g., why they chose to work the job they do and what about it that excites them the most).

How to Improve Your Small-Talk Skills

Meeting new people, networking, or spreading your influence hardly ever goes without some small talk. When you don't know new people well, the only suitable topics to talk about are those you have in common, which aren't many in this situation. Not everyone likes small talk, but it's necessary to develop deeper bonds and connections. You may think of small talks as trivial conversations, but they're anything but that. They are necessary to discover common interests with other people, and they lead to more meaningful conversations that people enjoy the most. But how do you become successful with small talk?

1. Be comfortable with yourself first. If you spend minutes or even hours leading up to the event, obsessing over having to chat and meet new people, this will shift your focus from the real purpose of the occasion. Instead, think about why you're going to the event in the first place. Think about the goals and how you want to present yourself. If it's a happy, more relaxed occasion (e.g., a wedding), think about those people whose friendship you're honoring by going to the event and how all people you'll meet there are important to them.

2. Think about people you know who will attend the same event. Meeting new people is

How to be Charismatic & Develop Confidence

a lot easier when there's someone you know to keep you company. Think about the people you have something in common with, and plan to approach them when you arrive at the event.

3. Make it fun. One of the best ways to do small talk is to make a challenge out of it. Set your mind to meet a certain number of new people and spend a specific amount of time chatting. This way, you will be competing with yourself. Moreover, you think less about the anxiety and perhaps awkwardness that go into having these conversations.

4. Show initiative. If you wait for people to approach you, there are good chances that you might meet only a person or two or even no one. On the other hand, if you set your mind to approach people first (and even better, make a task or a challenge out of it), you will become more comfortable being introduced to new acquaintances. Here, it's important not to spend the entire event following the one person you know. Depending on your relationship (and particularly if you're not very close), it can become awkward, and the other person might feel stifled. Instead, branch out and meet other people independently.

5. Remember your task. Whichever event you're going to, you have a certain role. Think about your role and how to do it the best way you can. When you're aware of why you're there, this will give you a point of focus. Now that you know what you aim to do, think about the people who are the best likely companions, and show interest in these people. Aside from that, be approachable, pleasant, and positive. Be your authentic self. Remember, people are very good at detecting authenticity and won't like a person who appears to have a good time but, in fact, looks uninterested when they talk to them.

How to Lead Conversations to Connect and Spread Your Influence

Essentially, small talks are informal conversations that need a little bit of strategizing for those who are shy or don't like meeting new people. Here are a couple of suggestions for making small talk that can build rapport and network:

1. Be a subtle interrogator. Asking questions has been mentioned multiple times in this book. However, it's important to specify what kind of questions you'll ask during small talk. You see, it's imperative to distinguish appropriate questions for formal conversations and those in casual chit-chat. The former requires more profound questions that show your understanding and empathy, and the latter demands a more light-hearted, gentler approach. While chatting, you should ask questions that showcase a spark of interest. However, don't make anyone feel awkward or intrude on their privacy. Your questions should be more general and open-ended, allowing the person to answer in a way that says more about their lifestyle and personality. Next, your questions should be fun, relatable, and suitable to the occasion. It's essential to find something both of you enjoy talking about.

2. Take in the information. Aside from using the active-listening skills mentioned earlier, a casual chat is an excellent opportunity to notice things about people they're less likely to speak directly about. When you listen carefully (particularly during a chat), you can observe not only what the other person likes but also what frustrates them and what they dislike. Moreover, you can conclude about their personality based on that.

3. *Show you're interested.* Of course, showing you're interested by being actively engaged in the conversation and putting away any distractions and electronics is important to keep the person's attention and interest. Showing enthusiasm to get to know the other person is vital for them to feel comfortable. Most of the time, people worry about imposing themselves on other people, which is why they feel less comfortable chatting and are most likely to end it quickly. When you show genuine interest and make the other person feel important and valued, there's a greater chance that they will remember you.

How to Keep Conversations Going to Avoid Awkward Pauses

Despite having excellent conversation skills, many find it hard to discover appropriate topics for casual chat. At the same time, most people dread the moments of awkward pause when they don't know what to say. Here are some suggestions for potentially great small-talk topics:

1. *The environment:* You can discuss and comment on the scenery while making sure not to say something disrespectful. Saying positive things about the venue or location helps point out that you're somewhere pleasant and comfortable, which is an emotion the other person will detect.

2. *Hobbies and entertainment:* You can spark a discussion on what both of you enjoy doing in your free time—for example, watching movies, reading, exercising, or training a sport. Try your best to keep the talk away from discussing work, particularly if it's not relevant to the situation. Some people find talking about work stressful and may withdraw from the conversation because of it.

3. *Pleasure:* Whatever makes both of you feel amused is a great conversation starter. Food and art are also great options. Everyone eats, which means you can discuss the food being served at the event and move on to talk about favorite foods overall. You can also discuss restaurants and other places you like to visit. If the person you're talking to appreciates art, you can talk about shows, colors, mediums, your favorite artists, and so on.

How to Improve Conversation Skills for Memorable Conversations

As you can see, there are many topics to chat about that can be pleasant and fun for you and the other person. If you're still not convinced in the value of small talk, here are some more strategies to improve your social skills:

1. Talk with purpose. All conversations have a purpose, and so does small talk. While the topics you're discussing may not be important or very interesting, they serve to take the pressure off certain situations. Particularly, it reduces the pressure to sound smart.

2. Aim to make people feel comfortable. Pay attention to whether the things you say make people feel more comfortable and at ease, or they introduce tension. When you focus on saying things that are encouraging and display compassion, you can help a person feel comfortable around you even when the situation itself isn't comfortable.

3. Stay in the moment. One of the most difficult obstacles to overcome is to stop thinking about the things that bother you and just immerse yourself in the present moment. If you have trouble staying away from anxious thoughts, remember the fact that thinking about these things won't solve your problems. When an anxious thought appears, remember that there's nothing you can do about it at that moment. Hence, there's no reason why you should allow it to ruin an opportunity to make new acquaintances. Also, avoid focusing too much on your posture, tone, and the way you speak. This will make you even more self-conscious and break the subtle yet pleasant course of the conversation.

4. Aim to understand what the other person is interested in. This will prevent awkward silence and make it easier to find out what to say and which topic to bring up. To do this, ask not only open-ended but also more engaging questions that spark more complex answers—for example, what the other person likes about their career or what their hobbies or interests are. If the other person says something you find interesting, ask them about it, and inquire about specific details you find intriguing or amusing.

5. Follow up with more engaging questions. Don't let the conversation die after the other person finished talking. Instead, you can keep the course of the conversation going by stating your commentary, mentioning something similar that happened to you or that is relatable in some other way. Then follow up with another logical or interesting question. Participating in the conversation with your own observations and experiences will prevent the other person from feeling like they're being interrogated.

6. Share relevant information about yourself too. Of course, you don't have to share too much, but things like your name, occupation, a general location, and other information are important so that the other person has more details to remember you by. Many people are uncomfortable sharing personal details like their address or where their children go to school, and that's fine. While you should aim to reciprocate the amount of information the other person gave out, it doesn't have to be the same type of information. For example, if your acquaintance said where they go for a medical checkup, and you don't want to reveal this information, you can say where you go for a haircut or mention other details later in the conversation. Still, make sure that the course of the conversation remains uninterrupted and natural, giving information that seems relevant to the topic. Giving information doesn't only make you more memorable but also more relatable. It helps another person paint a picture of who you are and what you do, and you become more than a name associated with a face in their mind. This creates conditions to bond and keep the conversation going.

Summary

In this chapter, you learned that small talk not only leaves a memorable first impression but also extends your network and achieves personal and business goals. The following are the ways to do this:

- *Enjoying small talk*: You learned that to improve the skills of casual conversations, you first need to be comfortable in your own skin and just have fun. No one will talk to a person who looks like they're being forced to talk to them by a shotgun. If you want people to like you, make them feel like you enjoy being around them.

- *Being a bit sneaky:* Creating a bond with the other person and extending your influence will require sleek observation and evaluation of their character. Detect subtle cues and information about another person's character, motivations, intentions, and knowledge by observing how and what they speak. See whether they are consistent with their appearance and actions. This will tell you a great deal about this person's hidden needs, aspirations, and concerns, which you can later use to your advantage.
- *Being engaged.* Keeping small talk going depends on your skill to find common

and interesting topics. Using body language that shows your interest in the conversations, asking smart questions, and juggling different topics (common interests, backgrounds, the setting, and the social occasion) will help maintain the connection between you and other people.

- *Deepening the bond and staying memorable.* The goal of small talk is for the other person to remember you. This is best done by making them feel comfortable, asking open-ended questions, being present, showing interest in what the other person is saying, and of course, sharing memorable and personable information about yourself.

How to be Charismatic & Develop Confidence

Chapter 5: Storytelling

The main reasons why storytelling in leadership is so important are that stories inspire people to act, they help spread the word about you, your competence and influence, and they help people remember you. One of the reasons why people remember stories so well is that they are based on learning from experience, and our minds are hardwired to learn like that. Your listener's mind will want to remember what you said when you shared your experience, even when they might not be aware of it.

<u>Why You Need to Be a Good Storyteller</u>

Storytelling spreads inspirational ideas, and it helps demonstrate those ideas by using existing motivations and cultural knowledge to solve problems for a person or a group of people. These are the ways storytelling helps leaders:

1. It manages conflicts. Stories give an emotional, experiential background to what you're trying to say. When people are in conflict, they are emotionally charged and unable to receive direct helpful suggestions. The great thing about storytelling is that it helps convey a message indirectly in a way that is more subtle so that a tense, irritated person may find it easier to accept it. Because of this, sharing a leader's experiences has become an essential step in handling work and personal life issues, as well as addressing problems. At times, saying what you want using different experiences helps people accept what they don't want to hear because they are not the topic, and neither criticism nor instructions are directed toward them.

2. It helps plan the future by learning from the past. Leadership is all about following dreams, fulfilling visions, and accepting challenges and obstacles along the way. Storytelling can also be used to represent or visualize how a future with one's goals accomplished might look like. If you think about it, the best way to persevere through challenges is to have a truly vivid picture of what you're going after in your mind, and the best way to do this is to simply tell yourself a story. Apart from that, stories involve details (e.g., settings, events, characters, smells, and tastes) that help you feel like you're already experiencing the things you're visualizing. This enables you to keep your vision alive by being able to tap into the entire experience whenever you want to.

3. It influences people through the use of reasoning. As mentioned earlier, storytelling helps people accept things they otherwise wouldn't. This is because stories offer more meaning and depth. They create room to convey rational, reasonable messages that people may not like hearing but, in a way, creates an emotional response. When you try to pass your message using plain facts and numbers, there's a chance that the listeners won't relate much with what you're saying.

However, when you wrap this information into a story, it becomes emotional, personal, interesting, and meaningful. As a result, people remember the information they heard.

How to Tell a Convincing Story

Aside from knowing the right way to tell a story, it's also important to include the crucial elements that make the story convincing. The main aspects of telling a story that convinces people in your message will include context, metaphors/analogies, feelings, physical elements, and a surprise twist. These elements should be wrapped into a story told in a style that is suitable for business settings. These types of stories are usually told in a speedy, punchy way, with a positive twist or a funny remark in the end, if possible. Your story shouldn't last longer than five minutes, or else you might lose your listener's attention.

But how do you know which story to share with your audience? First, think about the key messages, projects, or experiences you want to share that are relevant to your audience. Which of your past experiences and projects are related to the particular situation? Your examples can include both successes and failures, as long as the lesson is relevant, useful, and beneficial to the audience. Other elements of the story can be used to enhance your point. Don't be afraid of investing time and effort into planning what you will say and how you will say it.

Being a great storyteller undoubtedly expands your influence and helps people bond with you.

How to be Charismatic & Develop Confidence

It makes you more relatable and personable. Knowing how to tell and share stories can make you an attention magnet and become a tool you can use to meet new people and spread your message more effectively. It can help you connect with a group and establish yourself as a leader. Here are a couple of elements of storytelling to keep in mind:

The story arc: This is the first element of storytelling to master. It includes saying the details that build up the story and create interest and intrigue, adding a twist to make a story memorable. When you're building up a story, focus on starting with casual details so that the tension, or the point of conflict, sounds more interesting. Include details of how you felt being in a particular setting or a situation that led up to the event in question. Describe how you felt, what you did, and what the other characters of the plot did. These details help you paint a picture of what you're talking about, making it more vivid in the minds of those who listen.

The hook: There has to be an element that will spark the listener's interest to stay engaged throughout the story. Whether it's a funny story or a tense one, adding the hook will build up people's attention before you add a plot twist. To make the story more memorable, act a bit out of character, and emphasize certain peculiarities about people's mannerisms and personality. Of course, make sure you're not disrespectful or offensive. Depending on the situation, you can decide whether or not to imitate accents, body language, and other little kinks that could add to the appeal of the story.

How to be Charismatic & Develop Confidence

However, make sure not to overuse these elements, or else you could come across as being fake or over the top. Unless you're making a career doing stand-up comedy, keep in mind that you still want to stay authentic and relatable.

The punchline: This will be the highlight of the story, and it will summarize its entire message and vibe into one or two sentences. One of my favorite comedians, Kevin Hart, once told a story that perhaps wouldn't be at all funny hadn't he imitated the posture of an ostrich. Essentially, Kevin told a simple story of how his friend threw a can at the bird, and it got angry. But he kept repeating how the bird's body pointed forwards and his head sideways. As he narrated how the ostrich came after him and his friend, Kevin's punchline (with an imitation) was

How to be Charismatic & Develop Confidence

"Its body was like this [standing straight and turning its side to the audience], but its head was like THIS [turns his head toward the audience with an angry, blank expression on this face]." To this day, I can't rationally explain what's particularly funny about this joke, but I keep rewatching Kevin time after time because I just want to get to that part of the story.

What can we learn from this example? Kevin used this punchline to paint a picture of the entire ridiculousness of the situation and show how it unveiled differently from what was expected. The punchline set the stage for the twist, which was you can't run away from an angry ostrich, not even in a car. The bird kept chasing the two men while they were driving away, and the joke ended on an ambiguous note. Did it ever catch them? The twist to the story is the element of surprise that completely changes the direction of the story.

As you can see, there's nothing particularly hard or complicated about good storytelling. Still, you might need some exercise if you're not particularly keen on being the center of attention. Attune your humor or drama style to that of the audience.

Being a good storyteller is essential because all leaders build their charisma around their experiences, whether it's success or failure. Those who look up to you do so because of what you represent and how your experiences relate to theirs; it's not necessarily about who you are. The best way to connect and engage with those around you is to tell stories that spark interest, motivate, and inspire.

How to Make Your Story Memorable

In leadership, stories have a role of enlightening the mood, reliving a situation, appealing to potential followers, and gaining their approval. In a nutshell, if you want to win people over, your story needs to become their story.

The first criterion for this is that the story is interesting. The topic and the events need to be relevant to your group and appropriate for the occasion. Here, you need to use smart, well-thought-through exaggerations in strategically chosen places to win over the audience. Too few, and your story won't be memorable. Too many, and your listeners will miss the main point.

As someone striving to become a charismatic leader, you should have multiple stories

How to be Charismatic & Develop Confidence

prepared beforehand for the situations in which you'll be asked to tell a story. Think about the potentially inspiring events from your life and career. Figure out the ways to tell them things that are positive, charming, and entertaining but still realistic and authentic. Leave out those parts that seem irrelevant or have proven to be irrelevant for the main point of the story.

To showcase charisma, you'll need to develop a talent for making an average story great. People tend to get excited about stories that mix sad with humorous events, as those feel more realistic and personable. The main point of your story should be clearly stated at the end of it, although it's a good idea to make the audience look back and try to establish the connection between the events they were told about. As you take your listeners through the most important lessons from your story, keep them engaged using humor and detailed verbal description of how you felt in a situation and what made you feel like that.

Another important thing to focus on is to know how to use your voice in terms of narration, tone, pauses, pace, and emphasis on words that reflect the most relevant aspects of the story. Being prepared, looking put together, and memorizing your story in advance will help you engage more with your listeners because you won't have to stop to remember what you wanted to say. Also, you won't disengage because you're talking while remembering what to say next at the same time.

Body language is another important element of storytelling. Your head, eyes, posture, hands, and legs need to move along with the story and reflect its emotion and course. You should add an element of drama to your performance but still in a leveled, authentic way. If your goal is for your listeners to remember your story as a realistic, relatable one and not observe it similarly to an acting performance, you should use these elements strategically to emphasize important aspects of the story. Body language, in this case, only serves to reinforce the story and not necessarily become the main focus.

In terms of learning how to grow your charisma, storytelling serves to help you break out of your comfort zone. It helps you grow and develop confidence and convert your own feelings to another person. If you feel nervous about being in front of other people, it is very likely that other people will also pick up on your feelings.

How to be Charismatic & Develop Confidence

They will feel nervous around you and may even avoid being around you. However, if you feel good and confident, you will radiate this feeling, and people will pick up on that as well.

How to Tell Personal Stories

People will want to be around you if you make them feel good, and that's the truth. By learning how to be a good storyteller, you will learn how to influence people's emotions as well. However, you will only achieve this if your story appears believable and authentic. It should spark genuine interest. But how do you do this?

First, look back at your *experiences*. Think about the most important and most memorable success, failure, happy, and sad stories you can remember. Your stories will have to have a correct, truthful, genuine base that you will later embellish to prove a point and trigger different feelings.

Once you find stories you want to showcase, polish them to *make them more memorable*. Here, you will work on recalling the details about the settings and people who participate in the events. Add context, like telling more about your background and how that affected the events. These elements will add impact to the story and make it more memorable.

After you've done that, think about the *structure* of your story for a while. Each story has three main parts, which include the context (the beginning), the conflict (the middle), and the resolution (the end). The beginning will serve to present the listener with the context, background, settings, and character. In the middle part of your story, you will introduce obstacles and twists. Then you move to the resolution. You will resolve the story in the end, where you'll explain how the characters got or didn't get what they want.

When thinking about telling great stories, you should *focus on obstacles* that came in the way of either you or other characters achieving their goal. This will help engage the listeners emotionally. Each obstacle should have a potential solution, and it is up to you to decide whether or not it is a successful one. Most appealing stories have obstacles whose surpassing usually leads to further twists. Sometimes these obstacles have both positive and negative results.

Finally, it's time to focus on how you tell your

story. When you're telling a story in person, it should be shorter because the listeners are likely to lose their interest after a while. Only tell the essential parts of the story using carefully chosen elements of embellishment and drama to truly highlight the most important elements. For this, it's important to use expressions of emotion and pauses thoughtfully. This emphasizes the message and maximizes emotional engagement. How you'll use these elements depends on the story itself.

Summary

In this chapter, you learned how to be a captivating storyteller to influence people around you and get your message across. You learned the following:

- You need to be a good storyteller if you want people to be influenced by your message. You learned that storytelling is a must in leadership, and it helps people associate memories and feelings with your message. It also helps them remember you and connect on a deeper level.
- You need to tell a convincing story if you want people to believe what you're saying. You learned that to be compelling, a story must be based on the truth but also embellished to make it more appealing and memorable. You learned that each story has an arc, a hook, a twist, and a punchline. These elements give structure to your story and help keep the listeners engaged.

How to be Charismatic & Develop Confidence

- You make stories memorable using tone of voice, body language, and examples that are suitable and relevant to the situation.

Telling personal stories helps not only spread your message but also establish yourself as a trustworthy, friendly person that people will want to connect with.

How to be Charismatic & Develop Confidence

Chapter 6: Presence and Magnetism

In one of the previous chapters, we talked about growing personal charisma. Now, we'll talk about taking your appeal to the next level. Magnetism is a quality that not only makes people like you but also draws them to you. It drives people to follow you, as they want to be a part of your communities and listen to what you have to say. But how do you become

How to be Charismatic & Develop Confidence

magnetically appealing to other people?

Magnetism is a quality that people with the ability to steal the spotlight possess. It is an attractive quality that can be used both for good and bad purposes. In this book, I'll share advice on nurturing genuine, authentic personal attractiveness that stems from a healthy mentality and not narcissistic or sociopathic tendencies to abuse others for one's own purposes. More precisely, I'll talk about developing the type of charisma that grows from a desire to love and serve your idea of the greatest good.

Some people are born with this quality, while others need to learn. Either way, in this chapter, you will learn how to develop a magnetic aura that draws people in. The first quality required

How to be Charismatic & Develop Confidence

for this is personal charisma. Charisma is often hard to describe, and it stems both from personal traits and from exterior looks and assets. Some people are attractive because of their looks; others for their intellect. However, there are also those whose personality is appealing.

In previous chapters, we discussed the methods and techniques for developing personal charisma and becoming more relatable. Now, we will delve deeper into this particular quality. Charisma stems from having a deep, healthy relationship with yourself. You will only be charismatic if you are truly confident and convinced in your own value and competence. Charismatic people are usually firm believers. Their faith and values shape their career and personality. Your faith and vision will reach and inspire those around you. But to do this, you first need to work on your belief system and your confidence.

Strategies for Growing Magnetic Charisma

Another essential part of being charismatic is to be charming. Now, *charm* is a trait that takes a bit more work. You must delve deeper into your character and discover how your inner potential to love and contribute to other people's growth can shine through your appearance and behaviors. This way (and particularly if your motivations come from an intention to do good), you will gain followers on your journey. People around you will want to work with you to help fulfill your cause because they see it as their own. Your charm can serve as a powerful tool for motivation and creativity. To do this, you can use a couple of different strategies:

1. Be polished and put together. Charismatic leaders always look and behave their best. Since they have a highly developed self-awareness, they are able to manage their feelings and thoughts in a way that allows them to control what they'll focus on and what they'll think about. As they're in touch with their inner selves, true charismatic leaders are never arrogant or egocentric. Instead, they have a purpose in mind, and they only display those parts of themselves that agree with their purpose. Of course, no one is flawless, and we're all people. However, those who strive toward being leaders carefully choose when and how to open up and speak about their issues. In other words, they confide in their friends behind closed doors.

2. *Focus on others.* Leaders are often in the spotlight, but their focus is on other people. This way, the energy between them and their followers becomes reciprocal. For this reason, their followers stick around. If you think about it, when leaders focus on solving others' problems, they give their energy to them. In return, their followers reciprocate but put in the work that serves the leader's purpose. Of course, it is always possible for this pattern to become manipulative or even criminal. Genuine leaders are led by the motivation to change this world and the people around them for the better.

3. *Develop your conversation skills.* People who possess a magnetic appeal have excellent *conversation* skills. They balance listening and speaking carefully. First, they listen to what others have to say and then respond with well-thought-out stories that share their wisdom, experience, and useful knowledge. Everything they say has a purpose, even if they talk about their passion, hobbies, and interests. Charismatic leaders are skillful storytellers who use their language skills and mannerisms to convey powerful messages. For this, they engage only in profound, meaningful, and important topics, avoiding offensive and controversial issues.

4. Pay attention to nonverbal language. Charismatic leaders pay attention to others' nonverbal language. What we detect from body language has a subliminal impact on the interaction. It affects how we feel and what we deduce from the conversation. Assertive body language, good eye contact, and carefully strategized physical contact are all tools that charismatic leaders use to connect with their followers.

5. Develop empathy. *Empathy* is an essential power behind authentic charisma. People are drawn to those who love and feel for them on instinct. However, where this connection will go (whether or not it will be healthy, productive, and growth-supportive) depends on how you wield it. Being empathetic means knowing how to put yourself in others' shoes and knowing what's healthy, appropriate, and helpful.

How to Influence People with Your Magnetic Presence

Charisma is a trait that can get you far in life. It can help you land jobs, conquer the love of your life, and find your way out of a speeding ticket. Some people say it even gets them free pizza every once in a while. However, rarely anyone is simply born with this trait. People who are raised to have strong confidence and self-respect may show it even as toddlers. In contrast, others become charismatic later in life once they realize where their true passions and devotions lie and become aware of their infinite value.

Scientists are yet to unveil the mystery behind charisma. What we know is that it is a learned behavior. It's not a gene that you are gifted with

How to be Charismatic & Develop Confidence

that makes you famous and loved. The so-called charisma is learned early in life and has a significant impact on one's success in adulthood.

No matter how objective and unbiased the modern world strives to be, charismatic people somehow manage to appeal to those who are in deciding positions, earning business opportunities and promotions that don't always stem strictly from their skillset or credentials. This is because charismatic people know how to influence people. Oftentimes, this knowledge is instinctive, and these people are good at noticing how to behave and what to say to ease other people into giving them what they want. This quality is highly effective in industries related to sales, art, and creativity, wherein appealing to people's unspoken needs and feelings plays a deciding role in making a profit.

Those who've studied charisma as a trait have determined that there are three common traits that help charismatic people influence others:

- *Being down-to-earth:* People with appealing personalities are attractive due to their "present" nature. Unlike those whose mindset revolves around past regrets and future plans, charismatic people live in the here and now. They address current issues with boldness and confidence.
- *Kindness:* Charismatic people have a loving aura around them. Their warmth makes people feel comfortable and open up to their ideas and suggestions.

- *Competence.* Charismatic people usually have a great deal of personal power because they also put in a lot of work into nurturing their talents and abilities and take driven but reasonable action to profit from them.

But what is the one thing that can destroy charisma? The answer is self-doubt. People who have low confidence and insufficient self-esteem avoid eye contact and have a slouched, closed-off posture. They smile less, and when they do, it's usually only on the surface or out of nervousness. All these behaviors combine to say to other people that this person isn't someone they want to connect with. If you think you don't have enough personal charisma, there are things that you can do to change that.

How to be Charismatic & Develop Confidence

1. *Set your mind to be firm and decisive.* Decisiveness means to spend less time worrying about things that can possibly go wrong and more time doing everything you can to advance and improve. Taking opportunities whenever you can is also a trait of charismatic people. They don't give up on a job application because they're not sure if they have a chance. They apply for jobs because they want them and think they deserve them. Social intelligence is a secret condiment of their career success, as they use other tools to advance beyond their skill set and level of expertise.

2. *Be honest.* The second important trait of charismatic people is their *honesty*. They speak their mind, but in a way, that's helpful and respectful. Their honesty is one of the main reasons why people trust them so much.

3. Inspire others without boasting. Charismatic people enjoy sharing the stories of how their *potentials* and drive resulted in astonishing achievements instead of boasting about the accomplishments themselves. For example, a charismatic leader won't talk much about their current post or their salary, but they will talk about the number of hours they put into learning the skills needed to get there or finish a project that was valuable to the company's vision.

4. Encourage people to be in the spotlight. Charismatic people want to hear others' stories and inspire people to talk about themselves. If you think about Oprah, for example, her whole career revolves around helping people improve their lives. She has hosted hundreds of shows focusing on other people's problems and looking for solutions.

How to Speak so That You Command Attention

Influential people also enjoy talking about themselves. This helps other people associate with them and connect easier since they've already shared so much about their own lives.

Confidence is another trait of influential people. People don't find insecurity attractive, but those who appear strong and reliable win their trust quickly and easily. People gravitate toward those they can rely on, even if it's only mentally through a screen. If you learn how to communicate the right way, people will want to connect to your knowledge and expertise. While building confidence isn't a simple thing to

How to be Charismatic & Develop Confidence

do, it's not impossible either. Gaining experience in the areas of expertise and following your passions to express your creativity will build up your sense of competence and help you learn how to trust your abilities. This will take practice and, admittedly, can't be done overnight.

Practicing not only confidence skills but also other personal and career skills will help you learn how to solve your own problems as well as other people's. All of this combined will build up your sense of unique authenticity over time. Confidence also affects how you communicate nonverbally, how you carry yourself, how you maintain eye contact, and how you use your body language. For example, a good measure of eye contact can make or break a connection. Too little or too much is uninviting or can come across as unnatural and strange. But people with true confidence instinctively know when to look and when to look away, which makes their interactions spontaneously successful. They don't have to scan their entire body to convey charismatic mannerisms—they do that intuitively.

Confidence is also essential if you want to be a good listener. Insecure people often overthink how they look and what they're saying, which makes them come across as closed off or inhibited. On the other hand, confident people are truly present in the moment. They listen to what other people say, not only because they aim to influence but also because their entire mindset revolves around genuine interest for people's concerns and the values they stand for. This makes them great listeners and great

How to be Charismatic & Develop Confidence

in engaging in memorable conversations that leave people feeling like they've never had a conversation like that in their life. They are active listeners and go beyond just being quiet and nodding. They process and analyze the things they hear, and they are good at reading between the lines and understanding unspoken messages.

Aside from understanding what's being said directly, charismatic people look into the background of what the other person is saying. They check whether the details of their story are consistent. Are there things that are being left out? What does the omission of these details say about the other person? Is there insecurity or shame they're trying to hide? Is there a way to help them overcome these feelings? More importantly, charismatic people are quite good at recognizing people's needs and desires.

The more you study human interactions, the better you'll understand how people's speech gives away subtle details about their personality. For example, you'll know whether they're confident or whether they care about being loved and accepted. Moreover, details about what their insecurities are, and what they think about people in their lives, can all be picked up just by listening and analyzing what the person is talking about.

However, this requires not only listening but also observing. Much like Sherlock Holmes, charismatic people are good at noticing details about people's clothes, hairstyles, accessories, mannerisms, and other relevant details to find out more about their personality and lifestyle.

Charismatic people are also good at analyzing other people's body language. Body language shows how a person feels (e.g., whether or not they're comfortable, confident, or insecure) and much more.

Charismatic people also possess emotional warmth. They smile (but this isn't a form of a well-rehearsed smile), have an inviting glance in their eyes, and tilt in slightly as they talk. These are all results of their unconscious minds. Charismatic people tap into that inner sense of happiness and comfort they want to spread to the world around them, which also reflects in their body posture and facial expressions.

Now that you know what it means to be

How to be Charismatic & Develop Confidence

charismatic and how to get there, you probably understand that this is something you can't fake. True charisma comes from a strong connection with your inner self and, more importantly, a sense of unconditional personal value. It enables you to notice other people's infinite value, and it creates an atmosphere of trust.

When people feel like they can trust you, they will also form a lasting bond with you. This is greatly affected by your state of mind. How you feel about yourself is the ultimate mystery to solve, and embarking on that journey starts when you look into your deepest beliefs, fears, and desires. It takes looking into your own goals and expectations to truly begin appreciating yourself so that others find you approachable and personable as well.

Summary

In this chapter, you learned how to start nurturing authentic charisma to appeal to people and spread your influence using the following strategies:

- Being put together, polished, attentive, empathetic, and skillful in conversations
- Listening to people and paying attention to their mannerisms, hidden needs, and motives
- Spreading your messages in a genuine, measured, accurate, and authentic way

Chapter 7: Being Assertive

Do you feel like you're constantly sacrificing your time and effort to accommodate other people? Do you feel like you're saying yes when you want to say no just to avoid confrontation? If so, you're not alone. Most people are raised to think (even if only unconsciously) that saying no is something bad, and putting your needs and goals ahead of other people is selfish. While that couldn't be further from the truth, many of us overly accommodate other people.

Develop Social Assertiveness and Get What You Need and Want Out of Interactions

Whether it's business or relationships, many people think that having your own boundaries and preserving your integrity is selfish and wrong. If you want to become successful and influential, you're going to have to learn how to overcome this notion.

But how will you stop accommodating other people and sacrificing your time and effort to do other people's work or fix other people's errors if you feel like you're being selfish or irresponsible if you don't do so? The answer is by learning about becoming more assertive.

Perhaps you are unable to say no to your boss or return a cold meal at the restaurant. You must know that the inability to stand up for yourself can cost you and everyone else around you. If not in time and money, the cost is being unable to do your best work and focus your energy on the activities that lead to growth because you are doing mundane chores that are truly irrelevant in the long run.

Assertiveness Isn't a Personality—It's a Skill

The inability to establish healthy boundaries results from being afraid of disappointing other people and being rejected. And perhaps, people who don't stand up to their superiors at work fear the possibility of losing their jobs. Sometimes people will even sacrifice their

How to be Charismatic & Develop Confidence

hobbies and interests just so as not to let down certain people. These fears all come from quite innate fears of rejection. Once you realize that your fears have nothing to do with the prospect of real-life consequences, you'll start to look at these situations from a different perspective. Having a respectful but firm heart-to-heart with those who push your boundaries doesn't have to be inappropriate or awkward. It can be done in ways that allow the other person to understand how their behavior affects you, and more importantly, it conveys that your message and decision are final.

Being unable to say no sometimes means that you have the "nice guy/girl" syndrome. This syndrome includes numerous traits, behaviors, and attitude characteristics of people who take a passive approach to life, giving everyone

How to be Charismatic & Develop Confidence

around them the power to make their decisions and occupy their time and schedule. Oftentimes, you find it hard to say no even when the demands are unreasonable or harmful for you, simply out of fear that you will anger or affect others. As you may notice, this is most certainly not a healthy nor helpful trait. By being a nice guy/girl, you're not really helping anyone.

If you think about it, your behaviors don't allow people to see the true consequences of their actions. Beneath all this lies the problem with anxiousness and low self-esteem, which leads to building up resentment for people around you, even the closest ones.

Have you ever accommodated friends and family members only to realize you cringe as soon as they call and that you avoid picking up the phone because you can't stand having another conversation with them? This feeling doesn't always result from the traits of that particular person or their true toxicity. Often, your inability to speak your mind makes you feel as if the person has expectations they actually don't have. You're thinking about those individuals as intrusive and unpleasant to be around. The longer this lasts, the greater the chances of your relationship ending in flames.

The worst consequence of being unable to stand up for yourself is the reluctance to focus on your dreams and goals. Because you think (at least unconsciously) that other people will be offended and feel abandoned if you choose to focus on yourself, you sacrifice your dreams. As you can assume, this has little chance of ending well. It can make you feel stuck and helpless. As suppressed needs, feelings, and thoughts build, you eventually start to carry resentment. The more you feel like other people are taking advantage of you, the more you're likely to burst into a rage or even violence. Now, that's not a good way to go through life, isn't it?

To stop thinking and acting in this way, you'll have to learn to become more proactive and assume more control over your life. Rather than shifting from one extreme to another, you can start learning how to stay in the middle of the spectrum between complete passiveness and destructive aggressiveness. This position is also called assertiveness.

How to Start Training to Be Assertive

Assertiveness is more than simple confidence

training. Typically, men are taught to be more in touch with their emotions, while women are taught to be more confident. However, this is an oversimplification of what it means to be assertive. Assertiveness is a complex interpersonal skill of nurturing healthy confidence in ways that are respectful to both yourself and other people's boundaries. Being assertive means being honest. It means speaking your mind about things that bother you, as well as those you want or don't want. This is because you will stop assuming what people think. The more you realize how off your assumptions can be, the more you understand the importance of being truthful.

However, assertiveness skills also help you convey your opinion in ways that help find common ground. They don't leave much space for misinterpretation. For example, you'll learn how to speak your mind in ways that won't necessarily upset a person or hurt their feelings. You will learn how to communicate in ways that help reach a compromise. This way, you will understand how to go after what you want without fear that it will make you lonely or hurt those around you.

The benefits of being assertive are numerous. Being more assertive improves your relationships and makes them healthier. This will happen because you'll know how to communicate your needs in ways the other person will understand. This will prevent resentment from building up. Aside from that, you will feel less stressed. People who go through assertiveness training develop better strategies to cope with stress. As you learn to

How to be Charismatic & Develop Confidence

turn down requests that put pressure on you and focus more on doing the things you want, you will become less anxious. You will care less about what other people think about you and your opinions, actions, choices, and tastes.

Once you start learning how to become more assertive, you will start feeling like you're more in control of your life. This will help you start building confidence. As you know by now, it's very hard to develop strong confidence when your focus is on the things other people want and not those that you want. Don't allow other people to dictate your actions and occupy your schedule.

When you start paying more attention to what you think and what you want, your decisions and motivations come from a different place, and it's certainly not a selfish one. If you recall, I mentioned that charismatic people have a keen awareness of what they stand for. More often than not, their motives revolve around helping others while doing things that feel good for them too.

Oprah Winfrey has helped dozens. She runs numerous charities and changes others' lives every day. But she gets a spot on the air, luxuries of a convenient life, and social status. Kevin Hart makes people laugh but charges a good amount of money for it. Once you bridge the gap between wanting to contribute and wanting to make yourself happy, your confidence will start to thrive. But to do this, you first need to be aware of personal goals and be in full control of your life goals, which can be done once you become more assertive.

Being more assertive will also help you relieve anger and resentment. These feelings stem from your decisions to accommodate other people, and not necessarily from other people's malice and expectations. Once you become more aware of this (particularly when you devote to doing more of the things you want), you will become more tolerant and feel overall more peaceful and positive. As you can see, the benefits of becoming more assertive are numerous. But how do you get there?

Step 1: *Adopt an assertive mindset.* The first step toward nurturing assertiveness is to start adopting an assertive mindset. Your task will be to review your beliefs and let go of all inner limitations. The more you do this, the more you'll start to understand how your growth and happiness help everyone else. The more you observe how actions done in the name of selflessness are less helpful than those done for the purpose of personal growth, the more you'll grow a faith that setting healthy boundaries benefits everyone around you. It helps your business, your friends, your family, and your relatives.

Step 2: Start setting healthy boundaries. The next step in becoming more assertive is to learn how to start setting healthy boundaries. Healthy boundaries are a set of limits and rules that define what you're willing or unwilling to allow other people to do. The fewer boundaries you have, the greater the chance of allowing yourself to become a pushover. When you nurture your boundaries, your mindset will shift, and your confidence will grow. This will benefit your health, relationships, and career.

Step 3: Take personal responsibility. Personal responsibility is the other side of the assertive coin. You have *rights* on one side, and *responsibilities* on the other side. Here, I'm not just talking about daily tasks and chores. Responsibility (or better yet, *self-responsibility*) is the trait that helps you look at yourself as in charge of your well-being. People who lack self-responsibility view other people as both a cause and a solution to their problem. This is because they have a passive approach to life. For example, you might be unhappy in a relationship and think the problem is that the other person doesn't pay enough attention to you. But the real problem is that you rely on other people for attention and validation, and the truth could be that you expect more attention from people than they feel comfortable giving. As you learn to become more assertive, you will assume responsibility for your happiness and do more of the things that make you happy on your own. This way, you'll no longer expect other people to make you happy.

Taking responsibility for your problems and actions, as well as their consequences, helps you become more proactive and take action on those things that appear to need changing. Most of the time, people avoid doing the things that solve their problems out of sheer fear of failure. The stronger your confidence, the fewer your excuses will be for not doing or achieving what you want. Assuming responsibility for your problems will help you see how some of your actions contributed to the worsening of your situation, even if a particular issue may not be entirely your fault.

Learning assertiveness will reduce the expectations you have from yourself and everyone else. You will discover that people can't guess what you want and that you, instead, need to communicate your thoughts, needs, and desires if you're going to give people a chance to understand you. Also, you'll begin to see how acting on assumptions can cause a lot of resentment and hurt to both you and everyone else around you. You will also learn how to speak about what you want and how to voice your boundaries in a healthy way.

Aside from this, assertiveness will help you understand that you can't control how other people will think, how they will feel, and what they will do. This can dramatically change how

How to be Charismatic & Develop Confidence

you see relationships. This will help you stop submitting to other people's will and trying to make everyone happy. Perhaps, one of the most important things to learn will be that you are not in charge of making other people happy. You shouldn't set this expectation upon yourself, and other people don't have the right to do that either.

On the other hand, you will also learn how to voice your needs and concerns in ways that don't step on other people's boundaries, sense of integrity, feelings, and dignity. You will learn how to maintain a gentle balance between standing up for yourself and what you believe in and being respectful. You will have to make peace with the fact that people will be unhappy about some of your choices and decisions, but you'll also be able to live with it. However, as you're responsible for the consequences of your words and actions, you'll learn to observe, evaluate, plan for, and consider possible consequences when deciding whether or not to speak your mind.

Techniques and Exercises for Assertiveness

Now that you know why it's essential to learn how to become more assertive, let's dig into some specific exercises you can do each day to nurture an assertive mindset. While some people have a natural talent for assertive behavior and naturally instill trust and autonomy into the ways they talk to other people, others need more help in learning how to communicate to get along with people while maintaining and honoring their identity and integrity. The exercises given in the following sections will help you achieve your goals using inner strength.

First things first, you need to understand that your upbringing may be one of the reasons why you may struggle with an assertive attitude. If you were raised in a way that signaled that expressing your needs is somehow undesirable and burdening, it makes sense that you will proceed with these behaviors in your adult life. Being unassertive means feeling and acting under the influence of confusion surrounding your identity. It means acting on self-doubt, a sense of inferiority, guilt, and shame. Everyone has a passive side and an aggressive side, but learning how to balance those in healthy ways ensures a balanced attitude that will get you where you want to be in life.

Exercise #1: Self-evaluation.

Practicing an assertive attitude starts by *re-evaluating your expectations*. Whether you're too passive or aggressive, you probably have a negative expectation of what's to come. As a result, you act on this negative assumption even when it's inaccurate. At the beginning of your assertive exercises, it's not your behavior you're aiming to change but your thought process. First, imagine a potentially stressful situation. Think about what makes you dread feeling embarrassed or defeated. What is the outcome you're expecting? Now, review how expecting this outcome makes you feel. Are you upset? Do you jump to conclusions, or do you withdraw? What are the things you'll say and do in this situation? Last and most important, what are the responses, both inner and exterior, that you want to change? Do you want to handle a similar situation differently, and how?

Exercise #2: Emotional awareness.

The next step is to *become aware of your feelings and desires.* To become more assertive, start focusing on being aware of what you truly need and want. If this is repressed, you'll feel tense whenever you have a chance of doing something important for you. Additionally, the image of what you think you want might be exaggerated, creating an additionally unachievable goal. To do this, study all human needs (e.g., feeling safe and fed, loved, accepted, meaningful, and fulfilled). Next, create a vision board of how you see those needs manifested in real life. How should your life be so that these needs are fulfilled? Are there things in your life that you might be accepting or denying to protect yourself from negative feelings? Think about how the things you fear relate to those needs that aren't being fulfilled.

Exercise #3: Identify your strengths.

Everyone has some areas of their life where they're more successful in being aware of their needs and are able to identify emotions clearly. Think about your strengths and map out these areas. Recall how you think and feel in situations where you feel strong and capable of overcoming insecurities. How can you transfer these positive behavioral patterns into the other areas of your life? How can you take some of the useful thoughts, feelings, and actions from those areas of your life where you're successful to those where you feel challenged? Based on this, create an action plan on how you'll face challenging situations using the resources you used in cases where you acted assertively, and commit to putting your plan into action. The more you challenge yourself and practice these situations, the more you'll feel confident and competent to handle them.

Exercise #4: Process negative feelings.

The fourth step is to learn how to *work through guilt and shame*. While there are some situations you'll handle with more success; others will result in unfavorable outcomes. Perhaps your crush will reject your invitation on a date. Maybe people don't like seeing you setting boundaries. These are all everyday situations that happen to most people. They don't only happen to you. So ask yourself, how will you process the episodes of feeling embarrassed or beat down after facing an emotional trigger? First, become aware that feelings of anger or resentment often serve to shelter from shame, and it is the shame you're aiming to process. The best way to do that is to rationalize why and how the particular experience is nothing to be ashamed about. Mistakes and failures happen to anyone, and there's no reason for you to feel particularly guilty over any experience.

Exercise #5: Grow personal strength.

The final step in learning how to become more assertive is to grow personal strength. How is this done? The simple answer is by obtaining the resources of strength. What does this mean? It means to exercise appropriate body language, grow your social skills in areas that feel challenging, and learn how to process unpleasant experiences. The main reason behind conflicts in all areas of life is people acting defensively to shelter themselves from feeling guilty and ashamed. It causes aggressiveness, emotional suppression, avoidance, and many other unhealthy behaviors. Instead, practice using more mature, balanced ways to cope with challenges (e.g., using your own resources of gratitude, forgiveness, acceptance, bravery, anticipation, self-regulation, and self-sufficiency).

Summary

In this chapter, you learned just how vital

assertiveness is in leadership. You learned that being assertive means:

- Balancing your feelings, words, and behaviors to establish healthy boundaries, but also convey trust.
- Speaking your mind in a way that showcases sturdy confidence but also friendly flexibility. (You do this by reviewing your belief system, defining things you are and aren't willing to tolerate, and ultimately, assuming responsibility for your thoughts, feelings, and actions.)
- Developing emotional awareness of your inner thoughts, ambitions, and desires and identifying your core strengths and weaknesses.

How to be Charismatic & Develop Confidence

Learning how to process negative feelings and overcome personal limitations by reviewing how you thought, felt, and reacted in successful situations to apply these patterns to situations you find challenging.

How to be Charismatic & Develop Confidence

Chapter 8: Being a Charismatic Leader

How to Motivate Others to Be Excited About Doing What You Persuade Them to Do

Throughout the previous chapters of this book, we defined and emphasized the importance of possessing and exuding charisma to advance in all areas of life. As you learned, charisma is a trait nurtured through devotion to yourself and your core value system. It manifests in your awareness of what you stand for and expressing it with your body language, facial expressions, speech, actions, and appearance. For someone who is yet to start your journey, this is easier said than done. Of course, if living and acting on your best intentions were so easy, everyone would be doing it.

Without a doubt, journeying through life will require overcoming obstacles. Some of them are more obvious (e.g., gaining skills and competencies, getting to know people, and building your reputation). However, being at the very top of the ladder (a spot reserved for those who not only play roles in society but also build and grow companies and organizations and work to make a difference in the world) takes

How to be Charismatic & Develop Confidence

overcoming one more obstacle: learning how to influence others.

You see, your heart may be in the right place, and what you stand up for may make complete sense in your mind (and perhaps even in the minds of others). However, when you're working on spreading new messages and sharing original ideas, one of your tasks will be to persuade others to join in. There's a chance that individuals and groups who play an important role in the fulfillment of your mission may not see things the way you do, so you'll have to give them a nudge. Say you want to start a charity. You'll have to persuade people that your plan has a true impact on society. Or, if you're applying for a business loan, you'll have to convince the decision-makers that your business plan truly has a chance of success. For

How to be Charismatic & Develop Confidence

this, you'll need to develop the skill to influence.

Now, if your heart is in the right place (as it is the case with most people), there's a chance that you think that influencing is the same as manipulation. But what if it's not? If you think about it, "manipulating" means to give a false presentation of yourself and to use other people for personal gain. Manipulation is harmful to those who are being used, while influence isn't.

The key difference between manipulation and influence is that being influential doesn't abuse people's weaknesses and insecurities. Instead, it means wielding the power that comes from your integrity and confidence to convey a message people will believe. But it won't be because they're being lied to but because they

How to be Charismatic & Develop Confidence

trust your judgment and put their faith in your abilities. Much like the people you're aiming to influence, you too are being influenced every day. Either consciously or subconsciously, your decisions and actions are based on the trust in judgment and opinions of those you find trustworthy—whether it's your spouse, family, doctor, teacher, or a politician. So why wouldn't you be one of those people, and more importantly, how do you become one?

Being a charismatic leader means becoming a figure of influence. A charismatic leader, as research found, is someone who has a strong presence. On the other hand, being pleasant in appearance and approachable is a part of affability, which is the second key characteristic of charismatic leaders. As it turns out, people are very good at evaluating their level of charisma. Research also shows that if you were to rate how charismatic you are on a scale of 1–5, you would probably be right.

Before we delve further into this chapter, I'd like you to pause for a second and rate your level of charisma. Now, it's time to compare where you are now with the level you want to be at. If you don't think of yourself as being as charismatic as you'd like, there's also a good chance you know the reasons for that. What are the leadership traits and qualities you want to work on? If you're unsure which of the key skills and competencies need additional boosting, this chapter will present you with some traits and skills you can work on.

The key influences to develop if you want to become a charismatic leader are presence,

How to be Charismatic & Develop Confidence

leadership skills, and affability. This list may be short, but it encompasses a wide range of personal strengths, skills, and competencies to develop first.

Presence

Having a strong presence is the number-one trait of charismatic leaders. However, this trait encompasses four different characteristics to develop: confidence, self-esteem, optimism, and resilience. You see, as a leader, you will get all the perks of being influential. You'll get the spotlight and the power to make decisions, which will manifest in money, assets, and quality personal relationships. But with great powers come great responsibilities. You'll need to have the courage to step out first and fight for your goal, make plans, decide the right course of action, and accept the responsibility for risks and failures. This will take knowing how to predict and overcome obstacles and knowing how to solve problems.

Now perhaps it's a bit clearer why only a handful of people dare to lead. First, it takes a considerable amount of confidence to carry out this role. You need other people to believe that you can do the things you set out to do, and you need to believe that you're able to do them. Many people are good at convincing others, but not so much themselves. This is why indecisiveness, risky actions, and ineffective ones take place.

Your effectiveness and power as a charismatic leader grow with confidence and faith in your abilities. Your confidence, on the other hand,

How to be Charismatic & Develop Confidence

will grow with the ability to communicate across a variety of settings, groups, and individuals. Public speaking is perhaps the biggest challenge for one's confidence, and practicing it surely benefits your growth.

Aside from being confident, charismatic people are also optimistic. It shouldn't be difficult to understand why people want to follow those who built them up and not those who beat them down. So ask yourself which effect you think your presence has on the people around you. People are very good at detecting superficial, false optimism. Your task will be to nurture a genuinely positive outlook on everyday situations, even the challenging ones.

Being genuinely positive means making an effort to see the best in different situations,

How to be Charismatic & Develop Confidence

events, and people. However, to act in this way in all cases takes developing a good emotional compass and knowing what kind of positive outlook is appropriate for the moment. Let's say you're attending a meeting during which you found out that the organization needs to fire a certain amount of people. What's the right measure of optimism to use here? Surely, this is not the time to be overly cheerful. Instead, you can frame the situation as temporarily ending working relationships for the sake of long-term stability.

If you were the one to fire those people, what would be an appropriate thing to tell them? Remember, many of these people need consolation and encouragement. Many of these people would lose their jobs with loans and mortgages to pay or sick family members to support. If you were to practice charismatic leadership in this situation, what would you do? Undoubtedly, assuring those being let go that their skills, talents, and contribution will always be appreciated is the first step. It also helps to share a couple of supportive sentences about the direction they could take to grow their career going forward.

These would be genuine expressions of optimism in potentially defeating situations. How you leave things with people around you undoubtedly sets the tone for how you'll be seen in the eyes of those who you depend on. The fruits of being empathetic won't fail to show.

In the long run, positive communication helps you establish yourself as someone trustworthy and capable of managing problems, all while taking care of those who depend on you. This allows people around you to feel more optimistic, and you want that, whether they're above or below your rank. This is because those who are below you can push you up, and those who are above you can give a helping hand so that you reach the next level.

Both positive thinking and a positive outlook on events taking place, as you can see, create powerful tools in solving problems and negotiating solutions, whether it's at work or home.

While you can use your influence for both positive and negative purposes, keep in mind that the former yields lasting betterment for yourself and others in the long run, while the latter only has temporary benefits. The most powerful type of influence is the one that unites people around a common cause, and personal progress and benefits become only the side effects of it.

Leadership Skills

People with strong leadership skills grow and nurture them actively and on purpose, although it may seem that their charisma is God-given. Leadership is a matter of intent, decision, and action—first on self-improvement and then on fulfilling your mission and goals. Successful leaders use different leadership styles, all developed with hard work. These competencies help them convey their vision and messages in different settings and to different people, tailored around the circumstances and individual traits of those they lead. This is done using strong communication skills.

Affability

Developing the skill of conveying an attractive, inviting presence that inspires people to talk to you, engage in your plans, and listen to what you have to say is the third most important leadership quality. If you think of any leader you respect (be it Tony Robbins, Oprah Winfrey, or even Aragorn from the *Lord of the Rings*), what do you see these people having in common? They make you feel good about yourself, and they make you feel even better about yourself when you imagine being in their presence. You want to talk to them, confide in them, share your biggest fears and insecurities, and ask for their guidance on what to do to solve your problems. All of these individuals are affable. They all make people feel good and comfortable. But how do you develop this ability?

The best way to become affable is to work on growing your emotional intelligence. Tuning your emotional radar will help you understand people's feelings, motives, and actions better. It teaches you how to speak to them and share your message.

Another important part of being affable is being optimistic, which we thoroughly discussed in the previous section. But to have an optimistic outlook also requires knowing how to command your feelings so that your behavior doesn't come across as exaggerated or superficial. It will help you appeal to the best in other people so that you can direct the relationship toward what you want to achieve.

Aside from this, charismatic people are good at knowing when to show and when to hide their feelings. Of course, acting the way you feel isn't suitable or effective in all situations. In many of them, it can be quite harmful. Powerful leaders maintain a unique serene exterior, with the hustle and the work needed in growing their vision hidden from sight. This isn't lying, as it may appear. Acting in this way allows other people to focus on the essence of what you're trying to say. It helps to emphasize your key message.

Say you want to inspire people to follow your training program. Do they need to know you're struggling financially because of your student loan? Not really. Nowhere in your job description does it say they do or that it affects your credibility. So why would they have known about how you hustled to secure the funds for starting your business? Rest assured, they only want to see your rock-solid muscles and hear all about how to grow them with your assistance.

How to Quickly Read Anyone and Know What Triggers Will Influence Them

Being interesting to other people is another common trait of approachable leaders. A polished look and a smile on your face make you charming. The same is true when you have listening, communication, and storytelling skills and use appropriate optimism and humor.

How to be Charismatic & Develop Confidence

People want to be around interesting people. To grow this trait, pay attention to people's feedback. What are the most appealing parts of your interaction with them? Whether it is a public performance or a networking event, hearing people's impressions is useful to find out which of your skills are the strongest and which need some boosting.

How to Become Influential

Aside from the traits already mentioned (i.e., confidence, optimism, listening skills, and communication skills), here are a couple more skills to develop to become attractive to other people:

1. *Passion and drive:* Being passionate about the things you love and the job you do is inspiring. It draws people to you, as it appeals to their inner drive and passions. Being passionate gives meaning to mundane, everyday tasks, and being the one to remind people of that makes you a person they look up to.

2. Courage: Leadership means handling gigantic responsibilities, evaluating and making business deals, making bold decisions, and taking risks for the sake of everyone's personal growth and the fulfillment of the common goal. Learning how to be bold and brave means nurturing confidence and resilience to frustration, stress, fear, and failure.

3. Humor: The ability to make people laugh conveys confidence, but it also helps other people stay optimistic in the face of challenges. Learning how to use appropriate humor by analyzing the work of other leaders you admire,

How to be Charismatic & Develop Confidence

as well as your favorite comedians, will help establish yourself as a person people can turn to when they feel discouraged and need a confidence boost.

Now that you know why it is important to be charismatic, let's start practicing it, shall we?

As mentioned earlier, there are good chances that you can accurately evaluate how charismatic you are. If you're not completely happy with your result, you can start practicing some of the techniques to nurture personal charisma. The fact is that you can significantly grow your personal magnetism in a matter of weeks if you only practice daily and consistently. There are particular steps you can take to notice an improvement in less than a month!

How to be Charismatic & Develop Confidence

Without further ado, here are the strategies to become more charismatic:

1. *Let your inner self shine through your outfit.* Whether it's business attire, casual chic, or romantic flare, your style can do a great service to help you communicate your inner self. Before anything else, people around you will notice your outfit. The best part is that you can dress into suitable, stylish, and original outfits on any budget. However, the main rule is to only wear those items that spark joy. Whichever piece of clothing you put on, make sure it makes you feel happy and comfortable. Discomfort hurts charisma because people can spot that you feel uncomfortable.

2. *Practice eye contact.* Finding a good measure of pleasant, genuine, and appropriate eye contact will take exercise. To learn how to make impactful eye contact, hold it only a second longer than usual. The ultimate achievement is to maintain eye contact until the other person looks away. It might seem a bit strange at the beginning, but the more you practice, the more you'll build a habit of maintaining natural eye contact throughout the majority of the conversation. Only look away and break contact for purposes of thinking about what the other person is saying, pointing to an item used in the conversation, or taking a pause when speaking. These little natural breaks will help the eye contact stay consistent but not creepy.

3. Stand your ground. The art of assertiveness and charisma is all about making your presence known. For this, you'll have to learn a little bit about maintaining your territory, which subtly yet effectively signals personal power. You will start by taking slightly more space as you walk. Observe your stance as you walk the streets or enter a room. Do you shrug your shoulders and bow your head, mentally trying to make yourself invisible? Not anymore. Lift your head, straighten your shoulders, and spread your arms as much as possible while walking to feel more powerful but still natural. If you want to measure the ideal position, have your hands parallel with your shoulders, a few inches from your thighs, but with the elbows pointed outwards. As you walk, let your left-hand wave forward with the right leg and the other way around. This type of walk will help you feel and come across as stronger.

4. *Set your boundaries.* Boundaries are difficult

for many people, but most notable at work. This is because the workplace is an environment with more people to push them. While some people are good at setting boundaries at work, many are less successful in personal life, where they can't say no to friends and family. Either way, setting boundaries requires making it clear what you will and will not tolerate. Your job is to sit down and review what you won't tolerate from people around you. Determining your boundaries means deciding what's acceptable and what's not, and it's okay to have different standards for home and work, as well as for different people. Now, to practice setting boundaries, you also need to start making them clear. Learn how to voice your boundaries assertively. Make sure that your response is balanced with the situation and that you're stating a clear message without overreacting.

<u>Summary</u>

In this chapter, you learned how to develop the qualities that make a charismatic leader. You learned that persuasion isn't the same as manipulation. While manipulation preys on people's insecurities to abuse them for personal gain, persuasion resides on the art of convincing others to accept your point of view. To become persuasive and influential, you'll need to grow specific skills and qualities, including the following:

- *Presence and affability*: Presence means nurturing your sense of purpose and displaying it in your appearance, interactions, and actions. Affability, on the other hand, is a quality that combines friendliness, personal appeal, and relatability. To build this quality, you have to get to know people from all walks of life and learn to talk to those who have different tastes, opinions, and values than yours.

Learning how to read people to get what you want: This may appear as manipulation, but it can't be further from the truth. Reading people means finding ways to speak your message so that they understand it within their value system.

Chapter 9: Group Interactions

Communication is a widely researched scientific field and particularly well-studied in the area of leadership. It's no wonder since leadership mainly consists of communicating ideas, plans, messages, intentions, and motivation. As it turns out, successful leaders have powerful communication skills. They are able to appeal to people's most intimate emotions, send messages without causing conflict, and resolve disputes by sending the right messages. But how do they do that?

Communicating in group settings can become complex because you're working with a variety of different personalities, backgrounds, cultures, and individual character traits. For this reason, leaders tend to develop communication styles that are authentic to them but suitable to environments and individuals they work with. They understand that, aside from information, interactions also depend on beliefs, intentions, and motivation. They are capable of understanding why people say the things they're saying and why they act the way they do.

Group Interaction Skills for Charismatic Leaders

While there are many things that distinguish leaders and many situations that typically result in leader emergence, *communication, competence,* and *skill* are the primary traits that create the conditions for one to become a leader. Leadership studies that focus solely on communication skills reveal that people with above-average communication talent may emerge as leaders even when they're not in a leadership role. People with enhanced leadership skills are good at balancing personal relationships with tasks and procedures in a group setting. Typically, a person who understands and facilitates the dynamic of the group toward the common goal may emerge or be chosen as a leader. Below is a list of things

How to be Charismatic & Develop Confidence

that a good leader does.

1. *They contribute ideas.*

Good communicators make good leaders because they know how to *give, ask for, and interpret information accurately*. For leadership to be productive and beneficial for everyone involved, it's important for leaders to offer as many ideas as needed. This is because contributing puts them in a position of being evaluated by their group members, which strengthens the group dynamic. Whenever you're participating in group work, research shows that a simple way to grow your communication skills is to switch perspectives. On the one hand, give honest but constructive opinions about other people's contributions and ideas. On the other hand, participate with the same amount of ideas so that you, too, can get feedback on your work.

2. They contribute to group functions.

Now, from an interaction stance, leaders must contribute to group functions to be beneficial to the group. They should *seek, evaluate, and provide ideas but also ask others to evaluate their ideas*. They should be able to visualize abstract concepts and generalize concepts and patterns across different ideas and fields. These behaviors help the group work toward the common goal and become more successful overall. Still, most people have preferences when it comes to tasks they prefer doing, and they are more successful in some of them than others. Despite their abilities, leaders should still delegate and turn over certain tasks to other group members.

3. *They do their best to achieve their goals.*

Your interaction skills should include communication skills that are relevant for the group cause or its functioning. More specifically, you should be able to identify and *set goals, create reasonable plans for their completion, and be able to summarize and clarify all the complex tasks and procedures* so that the group remains focused on specific tasks. Group leaders are also good at creating an inclusive culture, and they help establish norms for how the members will value individual and group work. They create an encouraging, supportive, safe environment without criticism.

4. They guide intergroup communication.

Growing your communication skills will require guiding the communication process in your group. By contributing *creative ideas for how your group can communicate better*, you can establish yourself as someone who understands the group dynamic and can help the entire team communicate effectively. This way, you may contribute to resolving conflicts and help the group function better going forward. For this, you should nurture the following traits of group interaction: regulating participation, helping people evaluate their contributions, conflict solving, and assessing group climate.

5. They develop public speaking skills.

Not only public speaking but also successful group speaking is a part of every leader's communication skills. While public speaking may be intimidating, it comes with a significant advantage: you're the center of attention, and no one can interrupt you. When you're speaking to a group of listeners, you're free to express your message undisturbed. But when you're working with a group and your goal is to navigate the course of a conversation, your communication skills can be put to the test. Whichever type of interaction it is, you'll have to learn to overcome shyness first.

6. They face challenging people.

Speaking to different people is in every leader's

daily itinerary. It should become a habit and something you do well spontaneously and effortlessly. Interaction requires and strengthens confidence. Regardless of how confident you feel, in the beginning, learning to talk to different people will only help you feel better about yourself.

The more you talk to people, the better you'll understand how your speaking and listening skills, body language, and presence play a role in daily interactions and how all of this changes the quality of your life. The more you talk, the better you'll notice how problems get solved faster, how willing people are to help out, and how you come across in the eyes of your observers.

However, to master these skills, you shouldn't

How to be Charismatic & Develop Confidence

only talk to people you get along with. Instead, practice talking to people of all ages, genders, professions, and interests. This will help you learn how different personality profiles think, speak, and act. It's particularly important not to shy away from people who are challenging your confidence, whether it is because of a different relationship or because they intimidate you with their appearance. A lot of times, even people we admire can make us shy. This can be someone you respect or look up to (e.g., your favorite teacher or your boss) or even someone you like (e.g., your crush). Whoever these people are, overcoming shyness when talking to them helps you get to know them better, understand where they come from, and build your confidence.

As you get used to talking to new people each

day, you can try having longer, deeper, and more meaningful conversations. This is important to build your presence. You might think that popular people are those who never approach others but instantly become the center of attention. You couldn't be more wrong! Most people who have a presence show initiative to get to know other people, and they approach them first. As you practice approaching people, you'll also learn how friendlier people act when someone gives them positive attention. This will help you feel more connected with the people around you and increase your social circle. It will also make it easier to take the initiative and become more proactive.

7. They learn and stay informed.

Another way to boost your confidence when speaking with people is to beat insecurities with education. Your insecurities and nervousness could stem from a lack of knowledge, whether it is about the conversation topic or social skills in general. If you feel socially unequipped in any way (e.g., you don't know what's the most appropriate thing to say or which gestures are natural and suitable for the occasion), the best way to become more confident is to write down the reasons behind your anxiety and insecurity and then read and learn about the particular topics.

Sadly, many educated, talented experts never get to showcase their knowledge and skills in their best light. This is mainly because

How to be Charismatic & Develop Confidence

insecurity gets in the way of speaking. To overcome this, make sure to do some research before making important social contacts. At times, it would be about the conversation itself and other times about people you'll engage with or the type of interaction (e.g., a meeting, a party, a date, or a networking event).

The third thing you can do to stop being shy and withdrawn is to be active and engaged in conversations. No amount of reading and learning can compensate for practice, and the same goes for developing speaking skills as well. The more you talk to people, the more you'll practice your skills and become more socially competent. As time passes, you'll get used to interacting and be able to focus more on how to present yourself and share strong messages.

Summary

In this chapter, you learned that all leaders have well-developed group interaction skills. Below are some tips that can help you develop these skills:

- *Share ideas and insights, and contribute to the group in that way.* When your team receives suggestions from you, they will see you as a part of the group rather than someone who only manages the work.
- *Contribute to group functioning by focusing on the goals and tasks the group is ought to fulfill.* The best way to learn how to communicate with a group is to get to know its dynamics. Plain and simple, think of what the group is about. Who are its members? What's their character and expertise profile? More

importantly, what can you do so that the group does its job better?

- *Focus on group goals.* People will follow a leader who takes them to a place where they want to be. If it's a work group, the goal will depend on projects, tasks, and strategic goals. In informal groups, it will be education or entertainment. Either way, your performance, competence, and significance will be judged by how well you guide people to do or get the thing they came for.

- *Guide group communication.* Want to be a leader? Lead the group talk. Help people clarify their messages. Understand other members properly. Resolve their conflicts. In other words, be a mediator (more on that in the next chapter). Remember, a leader is a person whom people can rely on to look at the big picture while they focus on smaller, more manageable tasks.

- *Master public speaking.* Shyness and insecurity are normal for every person, but a leader must learn to overcome them. Focus on the messages you're trying to pass and back them up with strong body language, aside from working on your speaking skills.

- *Talk to people who test your values, beliefs, tastes, and preferences.* Only by facing those you disagree with while staying respectful will your messages hold merit. Aside from that, talking to diverse personalities will help you understand how people from different walks of life think and feel. You will also learn how to adjust your style and communication for your message to be heard accurately.

- *Learn about communication, leadership, your profession, and all other fields of interest.* People always want to learn something new and interesting. Being eloquent and well-informed, as well as knowing how to wrap it up in an appealing exterior and expression, will position you in other people's eyes as someone who is a valuable resource of knowledge and inspiration.

You're almost there! You got through 9 out of 10 essential steps to becoming a charismatic leader! In the first chapter, you learned how to navigate intergroup communication. But what happens when things get rough? Despite your best effort, there's always a chance of conflict. A conflict can occur either between you and someone else or between other members of your group. Your role as a leader will be to solve it. In the next chapter, you'll find out how to work through individual and group conflicts to contribute to mutual goals and mutual growth.

Chapter 10: Handling Conflicts

Conflicts occur naturally both in workplaces and personal life. Generally speaking, conflict is a collision of contrasting ideas, opinions, interests, or views on the same situation. As someone who strives toward being a leader, unity is one of the key values to represent, and unity will require knowing how to resolve conflicts. In this chapter, you'll learn what conflicts are, how they occur, and how to overcome or work around them.

Types of Conflict and the Best Ways to Find a Solution

Good leaders are good at solving conflicts. A conflict can occur in any group of people and for a multitude of reasons. Conflict occurs when people don't interact. They are signs that the relationships and communication in a group need some work. Wise leaders can use group conflict to open up opportunities for improvement and to move closer toward the common goal. If not, conflicts have the potential to cause many adverse business-related and personal outcomes. If you want to improve your conflict management skills, you'll need to start learning how to create a productive work environment. It is an atmosphere of mutual help, collaboration, and learning. In any group, members will work better when they work together.

<u>Why Conflict Occurs?</u>

Conflicts can happen for various reasons—e.g., differences in opinion to feelings, cultures, religion, attitude, looks, race, or gender. Conflicting positions, roles, statuses, and values can also cause conflicts. A conflict can also be a blend of different causes. Regardless of the cause, a good leader understands that conflict is a normal part of life. They expect it to happen and know how to manage it. While it is unpleasant, conflict is a necessary experience that helps people evaluate actions, decisions,

How to be Charismatic & Develop Confidence

and consequences of their choices so that they can have better ways to move forward.

However, people often avoid conflict as it can result in unpleasant feelings. Conflict can make people feel angry, afraid, ashamed, or guilty, which is why many people are prone to suppressing it. If well-managed, conflict can still contribute to the betterment of work environments. Research shows that there's a great chance that people will feel like they understand each other better, improve their working relationships, become more skillful in finding solutions, perform better, and become more motivated to do productive work if they are in an environment that's good with managing conflict. This way, leadership skills that boost workplace productivity don't only increase your personal influence but also benefit the entire organization.

Conflict can occur on multiple levels—e.g., between people, within oneself, and in and between groups.

Between people: Interpersonal conflict can happen between individuals with opposing goals or different approaches to their relationship. Different personality types can create differences in opinions and choices. When conflicts like these occur, it's necessary to compromise. Unaddressed personal conflict, if suppressed, can culminate in the inability to communicate.

With oneself: Intrapersonal conflict is the type of conflict that happens in the mind of a person. A person can have mutually conflicting thoughts, wishes, principles, and feelings. Unless addressed, these conflicts can also lead to anxiety and depression. Intrapersonal conflicts may affect other relationships as well, creating interpersonal conflicts. Talking to trusted friends and coworkers is usually the best way to resolve these conflicts because it helps you weigh your options and circumstances to make the best decision.

In and between groups: Conflict can happen within and between groups. When there are divisions in a group or when there are conflicting views, opinions, and values, it can create friction and a competitive environment. These situations can escalate as well and become very destructive. Usually, intergroup conflicts can have great costs, but they can also yield great progress with proper management.

Conflicts within members of the same group can arise due to differences in personalities, unclear roles, differences in workload, and other factors. But how does a good leader manage conflicts successfully?

Best Ways to Manage a Conflict

Collaboration and compromise are the two most successful ways of managing conflicts. Both of these strategies contribute to group progress and growth.

Collaboration usually takes a lot of time and energy because it's necessary to establish all the needs and goals involved with the conflict. This way, the leader can facilitate the resolution by discovering ideas that can create positive outcomes for everyone affected. Here, it's also important to identify those feelings that intervene with group dynamics. However, it may not be suitable in situations where a quick and effective decision must be made.

Compromise is another conflict-solving strategy that helps reach common ground. With compromise, both parties are partially satisfied. Neither of the parties wins or loses; instead, they get an acceptable solution. Usually, reaching a satisfactory solution is possible when two sides split differences, trade concerns, or find a middle ground. However, compromise can sometimes lead to manipulation and perception of unfairness. Compromise is the best approach for both parties when other solutions don't seem to work or when there's too little to gain and too much to lose for either of the parties.

Conflict-Solving in Leadership

Knowing how to resolve conflicts successfully distinguishes true leaders from those who only strive to be leaders. Unlike those who see conflicts as problems, leaders see them as an opportunity to introduce positive changes. One of the most admirable leadership qualities is knowing what to say and how to respond during conflicts. Those who avoid confrontation tend to allow tensions in the workplace to build up, which has devastating consequences on work climate and productivity. Here are a couple of examples of how leaders step up to resolve conflicts and get people on their side:

1. Validate feelings. When people come to you feeling frustrated or angry, it's usually because they've been experiencing something stressful for a while. On top of that, they could fear speaking their mind will make the situation worse. Successful leaders never ignore people's feelings. Instead, they accept and recognize the significance of these feelings and express empathy, which helps reduce tension.

2. *Suggest a break.* When a leader senses that someone (either them or the other person) isn't capable of talking rationally, they suggest taking a break before allowing the conflict to get worse. Taking a couple of deep breaths helps people see if they've exaggerated, and it also helps them pinpoint the exact point of the problem, instead of blaming their team, work, or the entire organization. Office negotiations can get heated, and depending on the industry, a lot can be at stake from making one over another decision. In situations like these, leaders help the members of their team understand how the actions of everyone involved affect the end goal, making the argument less personal.

3. Praise feedback. A lot of the time, people are afraid of coming up to say that something bothers them, whether it's a coworker or a boss. Doing this can be even more difficult in environments that emphasize positivity and creativity. Here, employees may start to feel as if they're being toxic or hostile by pointing out that there's something wrong with how the company handles their business. However, this can have negative long-term effects on productivity. When employees are not happy, the quality of work is affected, talented workers walk away, and productivity suffers. Instead, make sure your coworkers know that you value their feedback even when you don't agree. This will help them feel acknowledged, and at the same time, show that coming straight to you to solve problems pays off. On the other hand, even if you end up turning down another person's request, appreciating their feedback will make them feel better, and they are more likely to understand the rationale behind your answer.

4. Praise effort. Most of the time, it is the result that receives the most appreciation. But some contributions can't be measured by figures—e.g., a person's loyalty or engagement in projects that fell through. Don't forget to mention and praise these invisible contributions. When people feel acknowledged and appreciated, they're more likely to work hard and be productive than when they feel like the result is all that matters. It is particularly important to give credit to everyone involved in a project because it's not uncommon for only a couple of individuals to take credit for a result that took the entire team's devoted work. This is profoundly discouraging to talented employees who will start to question whether they will ever receive the acknowledgment for their contributions.

5. Work together. Motivating people to work together to solve a problem helps establish a partnership in the office rather than passing the blame. When people are encouraged to work as partners, they're more likely to assume responsibility for their actions. When people are made to feel like there must be a winner and a loser, they're a lot less likely to cooperate. In a competitive environment, people can start feeling like taking responsibility for their mistakes means they'll be seen as a failure, while the other person wins. This is very toxic and can get in the way of a healthy working climate.

How to Resolve Personal Conflicts to Sway People on Your Side

There are many ways for you to handle conflict as a charismatic leader. Many of these are applicable across a wide range of settings and situations. Whichever you choose, keep in mind that the very choice to face a conflict instead of avoiding confrontation makes a world of difference. While finding common ground might take some extra effort, people won't fail to notice that you are helping make the workplace a better, more pleasant space for them. Indeed, resolving conflict requires a careful approach, but it is always better than trying to pretend like it is not there.

When conflict solving is promoted in the entire organization, people no longer see conflicts as something dramatic. Instead, the entire team and staff members know how to cope with them, and they are capable of finding a solution that will be acceptable to everyone. However, to manage conflict well, you need to be familiar with the entire working system. First, you have to evaluate the consequences of people's actions. To understand how each of the participants contributed to the conflict, you'll have to understand the office climate, their process, and structure first. But, what if you find yourself in a direct conflict despite doing your best to communicate and work in harmony? Here are the crucial steps for winning in this

How to be Charismatic & Develop Confidence

situation:

1. Ask for more information. There's nothing more appealing in the workplace than a superior who truly wants to find out what people think about their work, whether or not something bothers them, or if there's an issue they need help with. Wanting to know people's concerns shows them that you're genuinely interested in your employees. When people feel valued and heard, it reduces tensions and helps maintain a more tolerant work environment. On the other hand, when they feel like the organization or the management doesn't care for their concerns, they're more likely to be less productive.

2. Prevent mistakes from repeating. As a leader of a business or the organization, you'll frequently experience different errors or issues. When this happens, it's extremely important not to pass the blame but instead do everything you can for the mistake and the negative consequences that resulted from it not to happen ever again. When you do this, people lose their defensive attitude and become more solution-oriented. On the other hand, when you insert yourself into finding a solution, you show them that there's equality in solving problems rather than a chain of command.

3. Find something to agree on. Acknowledging at least one point about which the other person is right helps them feel validated. When a person feels like they are being heard instead of being dismissed, they'll be more likely to participate in solving a problem. Being dismissive of other people's opinions only increases tension and anger, which further prevents resolving a conflict or finding a solution for a difficult situation.

4. Don't act like you know everything. Good leaders aren't afraid to show that they aren't familiar with something, and they demonstrate a desire to learn and hear more. These leaders get to see how a situation looks like from another person's point of view. Even if you think you know everything about a particular problem, there's always a chance that there are details you aren't aware of, but you would want to know. The more you ask questions and listen, the better you'll be able to understand the issue and find out what you can do to solve it.

5. Hold yourself accountable. Most people feel like the only way to win respect and credibility is to always be right, which is simply not possible. Instead, express accountability when you are being called out for a certain behavior. Being defensive isn't at all recommended in these situations because it takes a lot to win people over, but it's very easy to lose them. Keep in mind that people are coming to you with complaints they already believe to be the truth, and they count on their accusations being denied. If you justify their expectations, you will establish yourself as someone whose ego doesn't allow them to improve.

6. *Offer support.* Leaders who offer support, whether it's in casual conversation or during problem-solving, get to hear about the problems their associates, team members, or employees have. When you ask someone about how you can provide help and support, you make them feel acknowledged and safe, which can defuse conflicts and help people become more patient. This is particularly important in complex situations where it's not easy to establish who is responsible for a particular mistake or when people are unable to find common ground.

Being responsible when resolving conflicts will earn your respect among peers and employees. Your job isn't to be popular but efficient. When you're able to "put your money where your mouth is" and show people on your team what you're capable of, your popularity and credibility will grow. However, solving conflicts is essential here because conflicts affect the quality of work. Showing that you have problem-solving skills helps everyone trust your ability to resolve other problems as well.

How to be Charismatic & Develop Confidence

Often, leaders try to create a harmonious, pleasant work environment artificially. This means that they avoid confronting tensions but instead create a toxic environment for their employees. Essentially, problems are being swept under the rug. When things like these happen, people involved in the business lose trust in those they should look up to, and they start seeing them as shallow and greedy. How do you avoid this?

Using the aforementioned tools, you need to intervene right away. Perhaps you don't feel like you know enough to face an issue, and it could be true. Because of that, you should take a couple of days and talk to people to get to the bottom of a conflict. The more you do this; the more your associates will feel like you're taking their problems seriously. The work won't suffer as well because now that everyone in charge found a way to cope with their frustrations, they can start working productively again.

Summary

You've now taken the final step toward becoming a charismatic leader. In this chapter, you learned the following:

- Conflict naturally occurs between people, whether it's in the workplace or in your personal life. While the conflict occurrence itself isn't something to worry about, it shows that there's a lack of effective communication.
- Conflict can take place between people, in a group, between groups, and even within a single person. Causes for conflict can be differences of opinion,

conflicting interests, and other issues that call for the use of collaboration and compromise as a way of finding a resolution.

- Collaboration means getting people to work together to find a solution. While it is the best way to resolve conflict, it's not always possible. Often, people don't want to give up on some of their interests and motivations for the sake of achieving the common goal. In this case, compromise is the ultimate solution.

- Compromise means finding a middle ground. It is a solution in which all parties involved both win and lose something for the sake of achieving the goal. As a leader, you should compromise rather than use your power and influence to win. While it is possible to get what you want by using personal power, there's a risk of compromising your reputation.

Conclusion

Congratulations! You've made it to the end of your manual for becoming a charismatic leader. Now, you know the necessary skills you need to develop personal, financial, and business success.

The purpose of this book was to show you how you can beat shyness and anxiety to become a

How to be Charismatic & Develop Confidence

charismatic leader whom people will want to follow. We covered the essential talents and skills you need to develop for magnetic personal charisma.

For this, you first learned how to make a memorable first impression. As you discovered, first impressions are hard to shake away. People carry them around as an unconscious evaluation of your character no matter what you do afterward. In this book, you learned that to make a good first impression, you first need to adopt a confident, positive attitude. You learned that you need to be dressed to impress, and you need to exude confidence so that people remember your staple inner strength.

After that, you learned not only how to showcase confidence but also how to nurture it

How to be Charismatic & Develop Confidence

so that it's genuine and rock-solid. You learned the basic steps for training confidence. In particular, you learned how important it is to pay attention to your health, appearance, skills, knowledge, and values. You learned that being well-prepared for the occasion helps you beat shyness, nervousness, and insecurity. With this knowledge, you can proceed to share the best of your abilities with the world and no longer hide behind the fear that someone will judge you.

After that, you learned how to adopt a leadership mindset by becoming a good listener, remembering people's names, and making small talk like a true pro you are. You learned that, sadly, your positive traits, knowledge, and skills don't speak for themselves. Instead, you need to know how to

How to be Charismatic & Develop Confidence

present yourself to remain memorable and recognizable. To do this, you need to sport a polished appearance, listen carefully, and engage in casual conversations.

However, this is often easier said than done. As you learned in the second chapter of this book, there's a reason why so many people struggle with being memorable. It's called low confidence, coupled with a lack of self-esteem and often an equally poor self-image. As you learned, one must think positively of themselves and eliminate all self-doubt to nurture true charisma. In this book, you were given tools to nurture your sense of personal value and start improving your self-image. With the tools and exercises offered in this book, you can begin analyzing your biggest personal strengths and truly appreciating yourself for who you are unconditionally and without any doubt.

As you learned the importance of being confident, you also learned the value of building key leadership skills. First things first—you learned how to be a good listener by paying attention, processing, and responding to what another person is saying. These skills, while perhaps challenging to develop, will be put to good use the further you delve into building up your presence and making yourself noticeable.

Being a leader, as you learned, requires a reciprocal exchange of listening, speaking, ideas, and feedback. For one to become a leader, one must inspire. They must establish themselves as an authority figure but also a figure of trust and support. To build yourself up to that level, you need to possess the ability of captivating storytelling, interacting with groups, and solving conflicts.

To make a good first impression now seems easy, doesn't it? After the initial steps, the time came for you to learn how to inspire, entertain, and teach with your stories. You learned how to become a skillful mediator so that you can resolve your own conflicts and those within your team.

As you learned, for one to achieve their goal, they must know how to make other people work toward that goal. And what better way to do it than to understand and support their goals and motivations so that they reciprocate with actions needed for your progress? But on that path, obstacles may arise. You learned how to

How to be Charismatic & Develop Confidence

use your communication skills and body language to convey trust, capability, and confidence. But what if that's not enough?

Oftentimes, conflicts and heated arguments occur despite your best effort. Whether it's helping your team resolve their disputes or trying to work out a solution in a personal conflict, you found out how important it is to listen, appreciate feedback, praise contributions, and work toward finding common ground. You learned that, while there are obscure ways to manipulate people, the path that leads to continual growth is the one of understanding, collaboration, and compromise. As you learned, these ways of resolving conflicts depend on the degree to which people can align their goals and intentions. More importantly, you learned all the tips and tricks

How to be Charismatic & Develop Confidence

needed for detecting the invisible and navigating it to your advantage.

As you reach the final lines of this book, I want to leave you with a final message to not waste a second before you start exploring your authenticity. This is done through self-awareness and learning how to observe and analyze not only your goals and intentions but also your true capabilities. Once you realize where your true talents lie, you have found the exact strengths and valuable resources to share with the world. Your talents, skills, passions, and positive values are your most prized possession. They hold the key to dressing, speaking, acting, and leading in a way that works for what you discover to be your life's true purpose.

How to be Charismatic & Develop Confidence

Your purpose, which is unique and infinitely valuable, is what makes you a leader. It is your mission to complete, a battle to fight for, and a legacy to preserve. It is the spark beneath your shine and the force behind the magnetic appeal you'll possess after you've looked inside. Stay authentic, and good luck in fulfilling your noble mission of leading those who are willing to follow!

Get My New Books For FREE!

I love writing about personal development, and I am constantly in the trenches of writing a new book.

If you want to receive a **FREE COPY** of any future books I am releasing, please sign up to my free **VIP List** to receive your **FREE COPY**.

Sign up at:

https://bit.ly/RichardBanksVIP

Thank you for reading!

REFERENCES

Berry, D. S., & Hansen, J. S. (1996). Positive affect, negative affect, and social interaction. *Journal of personality and social psychology*, 71(4), 796. https://psycnet.apa.org/doi/10.1037/0022-3514.71.4.796

Cohen, G. (1990). Why is it difficult to put names to faces?. *British Journal of Psychology*, 81(3), 287–297. https://doi.org/10.1111/j.2044-8295.1990.tb02362.x

Diener, E., & Seligman, M. E. (2002). Very happy people. *Psychological science*, 13(1), 81-84. https://doi.org/10.1111%2F1467-9280.00415

Griffin, M. A., Neal, A., & Parker, S. K. (2007). A new model of work role performance: Positive behavior in uncertain and interdependent contexts. *Academy of management journal*, 50(2), 327–347. https://doi.org/10.5465/amj.2007.24634438

Klich, N. R., & Feldman, D. C. (1992). The role of approval and achievement needs in feedback seeking behavior. *Journal of Managerial Issues*, 554–570.

Mayo, M., Kakarika, M., Pastor, J. C., & Brutus, S. (2012). Aligning or inflating your leadership self-image? A longitudinal study of responses to peer feedback in MBA teams. *Academy of Management Learning & Education*, 11(4), 631–652. https://doi.org/10.5465/amle.2010.0069

Neck, C. P., & Manz, C. C. (1992). Thought self-leadership: The influence of self-talk and mental imagery on performance. *Journal of organizational behavior*, 13(7), 681–699.
https://doi.org/10.1002/job.4030130705

www.ingramcontent.com/pod-product-compliance
Lightning Source LLC
Chambersburg PA
CBHW020903080526
44589CB00011B/415